Clear Speech

Pronunciation and
Listening Comprehension
in North American English

4th Edition

Judy B. Gilbert

CAMBRIDGE
UNIVERSITY PRESS

CAMBRIDGE
UNIVERSITY PRESS

University Printing House, Cambridge CB2 8BS, United Kingdom

One Liberty Plaza, 20th Floor, New York, NY 10006, USA

477 Williamstown Road, Port Melbourne, VIC 3207, Australia

4843/24, 2nd Floor, Ansari Road, Daryaganj, Delhi – 110002, India

79 Anson Road, #06–04/06, Singapore 079906

Cambridge University Press is part of the University of Cambridge.

It furthers the University's mission by disseminating knowledge in the pursuit of education, learning and research at the highest international levels of excellence.

www.cambridge.org
Information on this title: www.cambridge.org/9781107682955

First published 1984
Second edition 1993
Third edition 2005
20 19 18 17 16 15 14

Printed in Dubai by Oriental Press

A catalogue record for this publication is available from the British Library

ISBN 978-1-107-68295-5 Student's Book
ISBN 978-1-107-63706-1 Teacher's Resource and Assessment Book
ISBN 978-1-107-62743-7 Class and Assessment Audio CDs

For a full list of components, visit www.cambridge.org/clearspeech

Cambridge University Press has no responsibility for the persistence or accuracy
of URLs for external or third-party internet websites referred to in this publication,
and does not guarantee that any content on such websites is, or will remain,
accurate or appropriate. Information regarding prices, travel timetables, and other
factual information given in this work is correct at the time of first printing but
Cambridge University Press does not guarantee the accuracy of such information
thereafter.

Art direction, book design, layout services, and photo research: Q2A/Bill Smith
Audio production: Richard LePage and Associates

Welcome to
Clear Speech
The world's favorite pronunciation series

Clear Speech supports students' learning both in the classroom and beyond.

With the **Student's Book** you can learn and practice how to:
▸ speak more clearly
▸ listen to other people more efficiently
▸ guess the pronunciation of written words

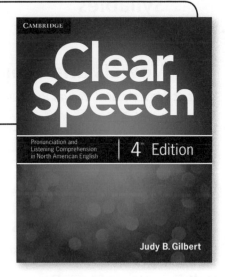

With the **Student's Book Audio** available at **www.cambridge.org/clearspeech**, you can:
▸ download the MP3s for all the listening activities in the Student's Book
▸ review and practice all the sounds and intonation and rhythm patterns presented and practiced in class

Contents

Syllables

Vowels and Word Stress

Sentence Focus

Consonants

Thought Groups

Appendices

Extra Practice 1
More Consonant Work

Extra Practice 2
Advanced Tasks

Scope and Sequence

Unit / Section	Featured Topics	Music of English	Vowel Work
1 **Syllables** pages 2–9	Introducing syllables Counting syllables Syllable number in past and present tense verbs Silent letters	*How do you spell "ease"?* *E-A-S-E.* *How do you spell "easy"?* *E-A-S-Y.* *What does "easy" mean?* *"Easy" means "not hard."*	
2 **Vowels and Vowel Rules** pages 10–17	Alphabet vowel sounds The Two Vowel Rule Relative vowel sounds The One Vowel Rule Contrasting alphabet vowel sounds and relative vowel sounds	*Did you say "hope" or "hop"?* *I said "hope." "H-O-P-E."*	
3 **Word Stress and Vowel Length** pages 18–24	Stressed syllables Rules for Stress and Vowel Length The Two Vowel Rule and One Vowel Rule for Multi-Syllable Words	*Excuse me. Where's the bank?* *It's on the corner of Oater Road and Selling Street.*	
4 **Word Stress and Vowel Clarity** pages 25–33	Clear vowels Schwa Contrasting clear vowels and schwa Stress Rules for Vowel Length and Vowel Clarity Identifying stress in multi-syllable words	*What are you studying?* *Economics.*	The letters -y- and -w- as vowel sounds Linking vowels with an off-glide
5 **Word Stress Patterns** pages 34–43	Listening to stress patterns Stress Rule for Two-Syllable Words Stress Rules for Word Endings Stress Rule for Two-Syllable Verbs Stress Rule for Compound Nouns	*Do they suspect him?* *Yes, he's a suspect.*	The spelling -ow- pronounced $/a^w/$ The spelling -ew- pronounced $/u^w/$ Linking vowels with an off-glide
6 **Sentence Focus: Emphasizing Content Words** pages 44–49	Contrast Focus words Focus and content words Focus Rules 1 and 2 Emphasizing focus words	*Follow that car!* *Which car?* *The yellow one!* *You look confused!* *That's because I lost my glasses.*	Review: Linking vowels with off-glides
7 **Sentence Focus: De-emphasizing Structure Words** pages 50–58	Focus and structure words Focus Rule 3 Contractions and reductions	*Do you mean the blue one?* *Don't you mean the red one?*	The spelling -igh- pronounced $/a^y/$ The spelling -oo- pronounced $/u^w/$
8 **Choosing the Focus Word** pages 59–68	Focus in conversations Focus Rules 4 and 5 Disagreeing and correcting Focus Rule 6	*You buy books at the library.* *No, you borrow books at the library.* *Our copier isn't working.* *Our what's not working?*	The vowel sound $/ɔ/$
9 **Emphasizing Structure Words** pages 69–75	Emphasizing structure words Focus Rule 7 Review of Focus Rules	*Our specialties are steak and lobster.* *Terrific! I'll have steak and lobster!*	Different vowel sounds for the letter -a- The contrast between $/ɔ/$ and $/ɑ/$

Acknowledgments

Thanks to the following people for their contributions to the fourth edition of *Clear Speech*:

The reviewers Eleanor Forfang-Brockman, Tarrant County Community College District – South Campus, Texas; James Kirchner, Vice President of the Michigan Translators/Interpreters Network; Stephen Peridore, College of Southern Nevada; Barbara Raifsnider, San Diego Community College District, California; and Kirsten M. Snipp, Tokyo University and Daita Bunka University, Japan.

My colleagues Barbara Bradford, Adam Brown, Madalena Cruz-Ferreira, Nancy Hilty, James Kirchner, Olle Kjellin, Barbara Seidlhofer, Michael Vaughan-Rees, and Robin Walker, for years of helping me think through fundamental linguistic and pedagogical issues.

Ellen Shaw for encouragement and guidance as editor of the first edition and for later pushing me to study what was known about spelling so that students could be helped to guess how to pronounce the written word.

Judith Alderman, for drawing the pictures of the tongue shapes looking to the front; Patty Blau, for her delightful interpretation of the happy hippopotamus; Dorothy Cribbs, for developing the original widened vowel font; Ames Kanemoto, for developing the concept of shrinking letters for continuants; and Jack Rummel, for his fine ragtime.

Karen Shimoda, Development Editor, who has been a much valued partner, helping solve the sequence and clarity issues that come with serious change; Debbie Goldblatt, Project Manager, for thoughtful review; Karen Brock, Senior Commissioning Editor, for her wisdom in decisions overseeing the development of both the book series and the Apps; and Sheryl Olinsky Borg, Publishing Manager, and Maria Amélia Dalsenter, Managing Editor, for insightful supervision during the finishing phases of these books, to make them as easy to teach from as possible.

And to all those whose dedicated professionalism has helped shape this new edition of *Clear Speech.*

To Jerry, who fixes things.

Letter to the Teacher

From the very first edition, *Clear Speech* has concentrated on the way that musical signals of spoken English are used to show emphasis – that is, stress, vowel lengthening, and pitch change. If the emphasis signals are clear, English listeners will understand the message even if there are errors in individual sounds. Conversely, even if the sounds are fairly clear, errors in emphasis or stress might confuse the listener.

Now the fourth edition of *Clear Speech*, revised with valuable feedback from teachers, adds new support to help you teach your students these musical signals of spoken English. The following pages of this letter outline the new features and how they work with the six basic principles and approach of *Clear Speech*. The letter also provides suggestions for teaching the different types of activities.

I hope that you find using this fourth edition of *Clear Speech* to be an enjoyable and professionally rewarding experience.

Judy B. Gilbert

New Features of *Clear Speech*, Fourth Edition

- **A pronunciation pyramid adds new support.** This concept makes it easier for students to understand how the various aspects of spoken English work together. The pyramid is divided into four levels, each with a distinctive color. The base, or foundation, level of the pyramid is the *thought group* (a short sentence, a clause, or a phrase). Within that base, there is a *focus word*, which is the most important word in the thought group. Within the focus word, there is one *stressed syllable*. The vowel at the center of this syllable is the *peak vowel*, which is the top of the pyramid and the peak of information. Accuracy is necessary when pronouncing this vowel.

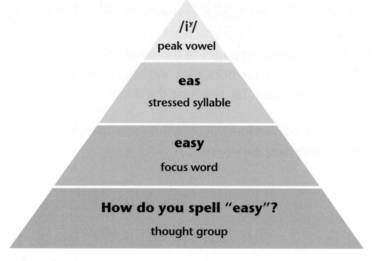

/iʸ/
peak vowel

eas
stressed syllable

easy
focus word

How do you spell "easy"?
thought group

Throughout the book, the pyramid appears at appropriate points to remind students how the specific topic being taught fits into the whole system of spoken English. With the same purpose, Rules and Vowel Work boxes are shaded in the pyramid-level color that corresponds to the topic being presented.

- **More support for vowel rules is given.** Sound symbols are used in specific tasks to help students recognize how pronunciation of sounds relates to the spelling rules. Also, the percentage of time these rules actually work is given directly with the practice tasks.

- **A four-color design adds visual appeal and clarity to presentation and practice.** A color design as well as updated illustrations and graphics make the presentations even clearer and provide more support for the practice tasks.

- **The audio program is available for students to download.** The complete audio program for the listening tasks in the Student's Book is available as MP3s on the *Clear Speech* Website (www.cambridge.org/clearspeech). Students can now download the audio for further practice outside the classroom.

Six Principles of *Clear Speech*

1 **Topics that are the most important are taught first.** This allows you to focus on the elements your students need most, such as how English speakers call attention to the most important words or which vowels need to be extra clear.

2 **Teaching points are designed to help students with both listening comprehension and intelligibility.** Tasks are presented with plenty of listening preparation before students are asked to speak. Words are presented both in regular spelled form and in special word boxes that show how they sound.

3 **Spelling and phonics rules are presented to help students guess pronunciation.** Vowel rule boxes provide the spelling and phonics rules adapted to English language students' needs. These rules can help students guess the pronunciation of unknown words and make them much more autonomous learners.

4 **Visual and kinesthetic modes emphasize key points.** For example, the lengthening of strong (stressed) vowels is presented in the following manner.

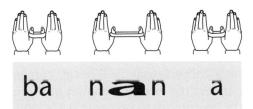

This makes the presentation clearer and more memorable for learners, especially visual and kinesthetic ones.

5 **Signals of spoken English are combined into simple, memorable phrases and sentences.** The Music of English boxes show these simple, yet common phrases and sentences, along with lines that illustrate the use of pitch for emphasis. Practice with these phrases and sentences help fix patterns in memory. A special color is used for these boxes, to indicate that all the levels of the pronunciation pyramid are being practiced at the same time.

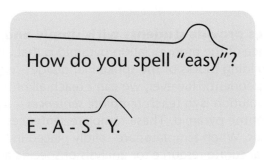

6 **Student pair work is emphasized.** This provides a communicative challenge and gives students the opportunity to practice not only speaking but also practice listening to different voices and pronunciations.

The *Clear Speech* Approach

The relationship between speaking and listening comprehension is made clear. Students who learn to recognize important signals of the natural rhythms and melodies of English often report improved understanding of speech on TV, in movies, and in face-to-face conversations.

English learners regularly complain, "Native speakers talk too fast." This often means that learners are unable to recognize the meaning of contractions ("isn't") or to notice grammar signals like the final sounds for plural nouns ("ticket**s**") or past tense verbs ("planne**d**"). Furthermore, difficulty keeping up with what was said also results from students failing to recognize the signals of emphasis or of word grouping. An example of missing the signals of grouping would be failing to recognize who is being spoken about in a remark like, "'John,' said the boss, 'is lazy.'" This is a quite different sentence from "John said, 'The boss is lazy.'"

Students learn how rhythm and melody are used as signals. In English, rhythm and melody serve as signals to help the listener follow the intentions of the speaker. These signals communicate emphasis and make clear the relationship between ideas so that listeners can readily identify these relationships and better understand the speaker's meaning.

Learners typically do not notice these signals that native listeners count on to help them follow meaning in a conversation. As a result, conversational breakdowns occur. Emphasis that conveys the wrong meaning or thought groups that either run together or break in inappropriate places make it difficult for the listener to follow the speaker's meaning. If the burden becomes too great, the listener simply stops listening. The principle of "helping the listener to follow," therefore, is a vital one. It is essential to helping students develop "listener-friendly" pronunciation.

Students are given rhythm training. It is not usually efficient to teach individual sounds without establishing some basic understanding of the English system of rhythm. People learning new languages tend to practice new sounds in the rhythm of their first language, and this makes it harder to get the target sounds right. Mastering the new rhythm will make it easier for students to say the new sounds clearly.

Template sentences provide students with simple and transferable patterns. The essence of the pronunciation pyramid is that all of the levels of the pyramid – the building blocks of the spoken language – work at the same time and are interdependent. However, we can't teach all of these elements simultaneously. The solution is to teach *template sentences* – the thought group that forms the base of the pyramid. These template sentences are found in the Music of English boxes. When templates are solidly placed in long-term memory, they can serve as an accurate resource for analysis of specific aspects of a flowing piece of spoken English.

Choral repetition reinforces the templates. The best way to teach template sentences is through *quality repetition*. Repetition, a truly ancient teaching method, fell into disfavor decades ago because teachers felt that it was boring. Repetition practice can indeed be boring, but *quality* repetition creates a momentum that is the opposite of boring and gives the students confidence.

To practice quality repetition, students first need to hear the template a number of times – in varying ways (loud, soft, whisper, etc.) but always at a normal speed retaining all the melodic and rhythmic features of natural English. If the sentence is slowed down, it will tend to lose these essential features. Choral response gives support to each speaker who, if speaking alone, might falter and lose the rhythm. The auditory support of choral sound and the strengthening effect of repetition give the students confidence and the satisfaction that they are mastering a useful template of spoken English.

Teaching the Activities in *Clear Speech*

Clear Speech was designed to be used in a wide range of teaching situations; therefore, you should feel free to choose those activities that are most appropriate for your students. You may also wish to shorten some activities if further practice is unnecessary.

Listening activities: Listening tasks such as "Which word do you hear?" and "Which word is different?" can help students learn to recognize particular sounds and stress patterns. When students practice hearing final sounds that make a grammar difference – for example, past tense such as "close**d**" or plural endings such as "book**s**" – both listening comprehension and pronunciation will improve.

Student pair work: The pair-work practice is particularly important, as it gives the students a great deal of realistic interactive speaking and listening. Pair work offers the immediate feedback so important to motivation. Moreover, it places more responsibility for learning where it belongs – with the student. While students work together in pairs, you can circulate among them, giving help on a more personal basis. To provide variety, the pair-work activities can be used as a listening exercise, with the teacher playing the part of Student A and the whole class playing Student B. Alternatively, one student can be Student A and the rest of the class can be Student B.

Additional rhythm practice: While rhythm is taught mainly through the Music of English boxes, there are also brief pieces of light poetry throughout the book, which have been included to encourage a sense of the flow of English rhythm. You may also find other poetry, or songs, more suited to your particular students. Rhythm practice is most effective when physical activity is included, such as marking time by tapping the table or moving the body in some way. The Teacher's Resource and Assessment Book suggests a variety of physical activities to reinforce the target rhythm.

Linking final sounds: Linking practice helps with listening comprehension, since words in thought groups typically run together and are linked as much as possible to keep the group together. Also, this kind of practice helps students concentrate on the particular sound being studied. Linking is shown in this book by linking lines within printed words or by running words together in the gray word boxes.

Another good use for linking practice is to choose any difficult sound, such as /l/. For instance, sometimes it is difficult for learners to combine "tell" with a word that begins with a vowel, like "everybody." It should sound like "telleverybody." The reason this approach can help with a troublesome sound is that it may be easier for students to say this sound at the beginning of a word rather than at the end.

Pitch patterns: English language learners usually do not hear intonation very well. When they listen to speech, they are powerfully distracted from paying attention to pitch changes because they are struggling to understand sounds, vocabulary, and grammar. The pitch lines in the Music of English boxes remind students of the importance of pitch patterns in English.

Dictation: One of the most useful general techniques for improving listening comprehension is to dictate sentences containing the specific element the student is working on. Repeat the dictation sentence only twice. Then give students the opportunity to check their work against the original sentences. This can alert them to areas of listening perception that still need improvement.

You can read dictation sentences aloud from the Teacher's Resource and Assessment Book or use the Class Audio CDs. Interest can also be enhanced by using dictation material from the students' own fields of work or study or from current topics.

Extra practice: If your students need additional work with problem sounds, use the exercises in Extra Practice 1, "More consonant work," at the end of the book. If your students have caught on quickly to the material in the basic units, use the exercises in Extra Practice 2, "Advanced tasks."

Use as many visual, kinesthetic, and auditory tools with these tasks as you can think of. There are imaginative tips from teachers included in the Teacher's Resource and Assessment Book.

Components of *Clear Speech*, Fourth Edition

In addition to this Student's Book, this fourth edition of *Clear Speech* also includes the following components:

- **Teacher's Resource and Assessment Book** with practical explanations for the rationale for each lesson, useful classroom procedures, teaching tips, more dictations, and short lectures for listening practice, as well as the audio script and answer key for each task. It also includes a listening diagnostic test, a speaking diagnostic test and a student pronunciation profile form, 15 unit quizzes, and all the audio scripts and answer keys.

- **Class Audio and Assessment CDs** with three CDs including the audio for all the listening tasks in the Student's Book and one CD including the audio for all the tasks in the listening test and quizzes.

- **Website** (www.cambridge.org/clearspeech) with extra materials and information about the series, including the complete audio for all the listening activities in the Student's Book as downloadable MP3s.

Key to Sound Symbols

	VOWELS		
Key words	*Clear Speech*	*Cambridge Dictionary of American English/ International Phonetic Alphabet*	**Your dictionary**
cake, mail, pay	/eʸ/	/eɪ/	
pan, bat, hand	/æ/	/æ/	
tea, feet, key	/iʸ/	/iː/	
ten, well, red	/ɛ/	/e/	
ice, pie, night	/aʸ/	/ɑɪ/	
is, fish, will	/ɪ/	/ɪ/	
cone, road, know	/oʷ/	/oʊ/	
top, rock, stop	/ɑ/	/ɑ/	
blue, school, new, cube, few	/uʷ/	/uː/	
cut, cup, us, rust, love	/ʌ/	/ʌ/	
house, our, cow	/aʷ/	/ɑʊ/	
saw, talk, applause	/ɔ/	/ɔː/	
boy, coin, join	/ɔʸ/	/ɔɪ/	
put, book, woman	/ʊ/	/ʊ/	
alone, open, pencil, atom, ketchup	/ə/	/ə/	

		CONSONANTS	
Key words	**Clear Speech**	**Cambridge Dictionary of American English/ International Phonetic Alphabet**	**Your dictionary**
bid, jo**b**	/b/	/b/	
do, fee**d**	/d/	/d/	
food, sa**f**e, lea**f**	/f/	/f/	
go, do**g**	/g/	/g/	
home, be**h**ind	/h/	/h/	
kiss, ba**ck**	/k/	/k/	
load, poo**l**, fai**l**	/l/	/l/	
man, plu**m**	/m/	/m/	
need, ope**n**	/n/	/n/	
pen, ho**p**e	/p/	/p/	
road, ca**r**d	/r/	/r/	
see, re**c**ent	/s/	/s/	
show, na**ti**on, wa**sh**	/ʃ/	/ʃ/	
team, mea**t**	/t/	/t̬/	
choose, wa**tch**	/tʃ/	/tʃ/	
think, bo**th**, tee**th**	/θ/	/θ/	
this, fa**th**er, tee**the**	/ð/	/ð/	
visit, sa**v**e, lea**v**e	/v/	/v/	
watch, a**w**ay	/w/	/w/	
yes, on**i**on	/y/	/j/	
zoo, the**s**e, ea**s**e	/z/	/z/	
bei**g**e, mea**s**ure, A**s**ia	/ʒ/	/ʒ/	
jump, bri**dg**e	/dʒ/	/dʒ/	

Clear Speech

1 Syllables

🎧 A Introducing syllables ☐☐☐

The basic unit of English rhythm is the syllable. Listen. Pay attention to the number of syllables.

☐	☐☐	☐☐☐
ease	easy	easily
care	careful	carefully
paint	painted	repainted
call	recall	recalling

🎧 B Tapping the syllables ☐☐☐

Listen and repeat the words while tapping your hand or foot for each syllable.

☐	☐☐	☐☐☐	☐☐☐☐
one	seven	eleven	What is that thing?
noun	sentence	syllable	I have to go.
can	cannot	continue	It's important.
can't	eighteen	direction	He wants a book.

🎧 C Which word is different? ☐☐☐

Listen. You will hear three words. Mark the column for the word that is different.

	X	Y	Z	
1.	....	....	......✔........	(fish, fish, fishy)
2.	....	....	....	
3.	....	....	....	
4.	....	....	....	
5.	....	....	....	
6.	....	....	....	
7.	....	....	....	
8.	....	....	....	

D Which word do you hear? ☐ ☐ ☐

Listen. Circle the word you hear.

	☐	☐☐
1.	mess	(messy)
2.	blow	below
3.	prayed	parade
4.	loud	aloud
5.	sport	support
6.	round	around
7.	claps	collapse
8.	closed	closet
9.	state	estate
10.	squeeze	excuse

E Pair work: One or two syllables? ☐ ☐ ☐

Student A: Say one word from each pair of words.

Student B.   I lold up one finger if the word has one syllable or two fingers if the word has two syllables.

Take turns saying the words. Do not always say the first word in each pair.

Examples

Student A: ˚ Sunny.
Student B: (Hold up two fingers.)

Student A: Red.
Student B: (Hold up one finger.)

	☐	☐☐
1.	sun	sunny
2.	red	ready
3.	flow	fellow
4.	rose	roses
5.	state	estate
6.	paint	painted
7.	boss	bosses
8.	sport	support
9.	blow	below
10.	sleep	asleep

Extra syllable in past tense verbs ☐☐☐

Usually, when **-ed** is added to a verb to make it past tense, the number of syllables in the verb *does not* change. However, with some verbs, adding **-ed** *does* add an extra syllable.

1 Listen to how **-ed** changes the following verbs.

Present tense ⟶ Past tense

☐	☐☐
rent	rented
plant	planted

2 Listen. Hold up one finger if you hear one syllable and two fingers if you hear two syllables.

fainted	landed	worked	caused	planned
laughed	added	folded	treated	counted
started	watched	closed	asked	cooked

Do you know the rule for when **-ed** is pronounced as an extra syllable? If not, try the following puzzle.

3 *Puzzle*: The verbs in lists **A** and **B** below have an extra syllable in the past tense. How are they different from the verbs in lists **C** and **D**?

A	B	C	D
plant	land	work	wash
start	fold	live	walk
treat	add	save	cause
wait	raid	laugh	plan
heat	load	call	close
attract	record	arrange	contain

Clue: Look at how the verbs in list **A** and list **B** are spelled. What do all the verbs in list **A** have in common? What do all the verbs in list **B** have in common?

4 Can you figure out the rule for saying an extra syllable in the past tense? Write down what you think it is. Check your answer on page 9.

Rule: ....

G Counting syllables in past tense verbs ☐ ☐ ☐

1 Listen. You will hear the present tense and the past tense of the following verbs.
Write the past tense of each verb.

Present tense	Syllables	Past tense	Syllables
1. paint	1	*painted*	*2*
2. clean	1	....	....
3. need	1	....	....
4. decide	2	....	....
5. dislike	2	....	....
6. prepare	2	....	....
7. represent	3	....	....
8. entertain	3	....	....

2 Listen again and write the number of syllables in each past tense verb.

H Pair work: Past or present?

Student A: Say sentence **a** or sentence **b**.
Student B: Say "Past" or "Present."

Take turns saying the sentences. Do not always say sentence **a** first.

Example

Student A: We wanted to buy a used car.
Student B: Past.

1. a. We want to buy a used car.
   b. We wanted to buy a used car.

2. a. The doctors treat sick people.
   b. The doctors treated sick people.

3. a. I intend to go shopping.
   b. I intended to go shopping.

4. a. People crowd into trains.
   b. People crowded into trains.

5. a. We start by checking the Internet.
   b. We started by checking the Internet.

6. a. We rent a lake house every summer.
   b. We rented a lake house every summer.

7. a. The teachers want a pay raise.
   b. The teachers wanted a pay raise.

8. a. They start at 8 o'clock.
   b. They started at 8 o'clock.

🎧 I Silent letters

Some English words have letters that are silent. Silent letters can affect the number of syllables in a word. It is important that you pronounce words in English with the correct number of syllables.

1 Listen. Cross out the silent letters in these words.

☐	☐☐	☐☐☐	☐☐☐☐
walked	business	vegetable*	laboratory*
planned	Wednesday	interesting*	elementary*
closed	every	differently	
talked	family		

2 Practice saying the words out loud until you can say them easily.

🎧 J Music of English 🎵

1 Listen. Notice the difference in the number of syllables in the two words.

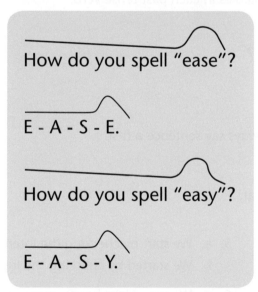

How do you spell "ease"?

E - A - S - E.

How do you spell "easy"?

E - A - S - Y.

2 Listen again and repeat each sentence until you can say it easily. Learn it like a little song.

---

* These are common pronunciations in North America, but some native speakers of English may say these words differently.

K Pair work: Asking about spelling

Student A: Ask question **a** or question **b**.
Student B: Answer the question.
Student A: If the answer is wrong, repeat the question.

Take turns asking and answering. Do not always ask question **a** first.

Example

Student A: How do you spell "easy"?
Student B: E - A - S - E.
Student A: No. How do you spell "easy"?
Student B: E - A - S - Y.

1. a. How do you spell "ease"? E - A - S - E.
   b. How do you spell "easy"? E - A - S - Y.

2. a. How do you spell "sport"? S - P - O - R - T.
   b. How do you spell "support"? S - U - P - P - O - R - T.

3. a. How do you spell "traffic"? T - R - A - F - F - I - C.
   b. How do you spell "terrific"? T - E - R - R - I - F - I - C.

4. a. How do you spell "squeeze"? S - Q - U - E - E - Z - E.
   b. How do you spell "excuse"? E - X - C - U - S - E.

5. a. How do you spell "boss"? B - O - S - S.
   b. How do you spell "bosses"? B - O - S - S - E - S.

6. a. How do you spell "close"? C - L - O - S - E.
   b. How do you spell "closed"? C - L - O - S - E - D.

L Music of English

English speakers let us know the most important information by using a rise in melody. This rise is the peak of information.

1 Listen. Notice the syllables where you hear the rise in melody.

> What does "easy" mean?
>
> "Easy" means "not hard."

2 Listen again and repeat each sentence until you can say it easily. Learn it like a little song.

M Pair work: Asking about meaning

Student A: Ask question **a** or question **b**.
Student B: Say the matching answer.
Student A: If the answer is wrong, repeat the question.

Take turns asking and answering. Do not always ask question **a** first.

Example

Student A: What does "easy" mean?
Student B: "Easy" means "comfort."
Student A: No. What does "easy" mean?
Student B: "Easy" means "not hard."

1. a. What does "ease" mean?   "Ease" means "comfort."
    b. What does "easy" mean?   "Easy" means "not hard."

2. a. What does "need" mean?   "Need" means "must have."
    b. What does "needed" mean?   "Needed" is the past tense of "need."

3. a. What does "closed" mean?   The opposite of "open."
    b. What does "closet" mean?   A place to put things.

4. a. What does "first" mean?   At the beginning.
    b. What does "forest" mean?   A lot of trees.

5. a. What does "traffic" mean?   It means "lots of cars."
    b. What does "terrific" mean?   It means "great."

6. a. What does "cracked" mean?   Something like "broken."
    b. What does "correct" mean?   "Right."

N Check yourself: Counting syllables ☐ ☐ ☐

1 Listen. Write the number of syllables above the underlined words.

This is the <u>first</u> <u>city</u> they <u>visited</u> when they <u>traveled</u> here on <u>business</u>.

They were so <u>pleased</u> that they <u>decided</u> to stay <u>seven</u> extra days.

2 If possible, record yourself saying these sentences. Listen to your recording. Did you get the correct number of syllables?

O Syllable number game ☐☐☐

Divide into teams. In five minutes, write the names of any foods you can think of that have one, two, three, or four syllables.

spagetti?
lasania

☐	☐☐	☐☐☐	☐☐☐☐
egg	spinach	Pineapple	pepperoni
rice	ice cream	banana	asparagus
cake	egg plant	zucchini	
beans	chicken	tomato	avocado
Beef	Dolma	potato	watermelon
Fish	Yongurt	blue burry	Matzarella
soup		lemonate	peanut butter

orange
steak
wine
beer

In five minutes, write the names of any countries and cities you can think of that have one, two, three, or four syllables.

Brazil
canada

☐ da	☐☐	☐☐☐	☐☐☐☐
Seoul	cyprus	Belarus	
France	Japan	Singapore	Argentina
	Maldives		
Greece	china	Italy	America
	Denmark		
Spain	Iran	Germany	Costa Rica
Rome	Turkey	Armenici	Dominica
Seoul	Russia	Albania	Colombia
	Egypt		

🎧 P Dictation: How many syllables? ☐☐☐

Listen and write the sentences you hear. Then count the number of syllables in each sentence. You will hear each sentence two times.

Number of syllables

1. He works in an interesting business. 9

2. ....

3. ....

4. ....

5. ....

Answer to Task F (page 4)

4 *Rule*: If the last sound of a regular verb is **/t/** or **/d/**, the past tense has an extra syllable.

2 | Vowels and Vowel Rules

A | Introducing vowels

In English spelling, each vowel letter can be pronounced with different sounds. There are only five vowel letters, but there are many more vowel sounds. The most common pronunciations are the **alphabet vowel sounds** and the **relative vowel sounds**.

In the following tasks, you will learn and practice the five alphabet vowel sounds and the five relative vowel sounds.

B | Alphabet vowel sounds

Listen to the names of the English vowel letters.

a   e   i   o   u

Sometimes vowel letters are pronounced like their letter names. These sounds are called the **alphabet vowel sounds**. The alphabet vowel sounds are pronounced with a small change in the sound at the end. This change is called the **off-glide**. The off-glide part of the sound is higher.

C | The tongue in alphabet vowel sounds

1 Look at these pictures of the tongue pronouncing the alphabet vowel sound for each letter. The solid line in the picture shows where the tongue begins. The dotted line shows how the tongue moves for the off-glide at the end.

2 Listen to the alphabet vowel sounds while you look at each picture and the sound symbol below it.

-a-	-e-	-i-
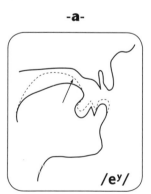	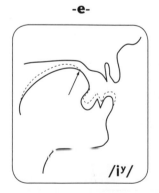	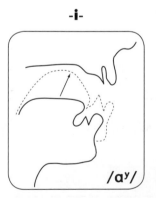
/eʸ/	/iʸ/	/aʸ/

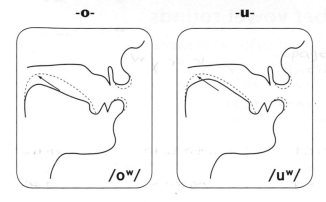

/oʷ/   /uʷ/

🎧 D The lips in alphabet vowel sounds

The following pictures show how the lips change when the alphabet vowel sounds are being said.

Listen to the alphabet vowel sounds while you look at each picture and the sound symbol below it.

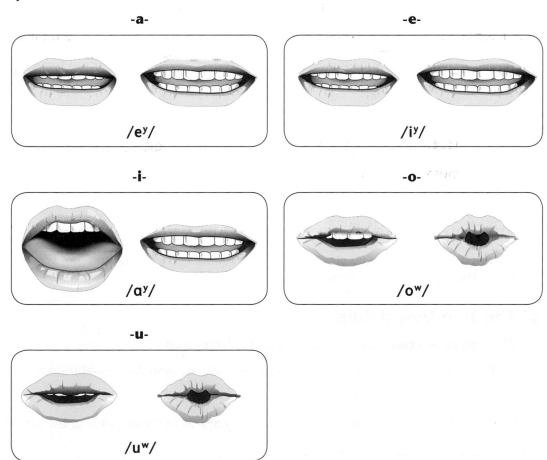

-a-

/eʸ/

-e-

/iʸ/

-i-

/aʸ/

-o-

/oʷ/

-u-

/uʷ/

Listening to alphabet vowel sounds

1 Listen to the alphabet vowel sounds in these key words.

(handwritten: & or ɣ w)

/eʸ/	/iʸ/	/aʸ/	/oʷ/	/uʷ/
cake	tea	ice	cone	blue

(handwritten: glide)

NOTE: The letter **-u-** is usually pronounced **/uʷ/** as in "blue." However, the letter is often pronounced **/yuʷ/**, as in "cube."

2 Listen to the alphabet vowel sounds in these other words.

/eʸ/	/iʸ/	/aʸ/	/oʷ/	/uʷ/
mail	leaf	lime	phone	tune
rain	steam	dine	coal	suit
train	breeze	file	froze	use
paid	feed	bite	coat	true

Which word has the same alphabet vowel sound?

Listen and write the word you hear. Then listen to the other two words in the same row. Circle the word that has the same alphabet vowel sound as the word you wrote.

1. ____tea____ (eat) ate

2. ____ice____ place (rice)

3. ____blue____ (suit) so

4. ____cone____ (coat) cute

5. ____cake____ (name) time

G The Two Vowel Rule for alphabet vowel sounds

This rule helps predict when a vowel letter is pronounced with its alphabet vowel sound. The rule works for many words.

The Two Vowel Rule

When there are **two** vowel letters in a one-syllable word:

1. The first vowel letter is usually pronounced with its alphabet vowel sound.

2. The second vowel letter is silent.

For example, the letters **-oa-** are pronounced **/oʷ/** as in "boat" 94% of the time.*

(handwritten: stone = oʷ   freed = iʸ   flame = eʸ   die = aʸ)

---

* For more information on this vowel rule, check Appendix C on page 144.

H Practicing alphabet vowel sounds

Listen to the alphabet vowel sounds in these words. Repeat each word.

a /eʸ/	*e* /iʸ/	*i* /aʸ/	*o* /oʷ/	/uʷ/	
change	teach	pie	boat	dues →	*charges, as for membership of a club*
main	mean	fine	chose	rude	
save	sleep	twice	note	prunes	
grapes	seat	dried	pose	duke	*British loyality*

 ## I Relative vowel sounds

Vowel letters are not always pronounced with their alphabet vowel sounds. Often a vowel letter is pronounced with a ***relative vowel sound***. This sound is related to the alphabet vowel sound, but it is different and has no off-glide.

1 Listen to the relative vowel sounds in these key words.

/æ/	/ɛ/	/ɪ/	/ɑ/	/ʌ/
pan	ten	is	top	cut

2 Listen to the relative vowel sounds in these other words.

/æ/	/ɛ/	/ɪ/	/ɑ/	/ʌ/
back	jet	sip	lock	cup
fan	French	pin	pot	jump
half	leg	kick	flock	fun
clap	send	wrist	clock	gum

J Which word is different?

Listen. Mark the column for the word that is different. The word that is different has a relative vowel sound.

	X	Y	Z	
1.	....	...✔...	....	(aid, add, aid)
2.	....	....	....	
3.	....	....	....	
4.	....	....	....	
5.	....	....	....	
6.	....	....	....	
7.	....	....	....	
8.	....	....	....	

The One Vowel Rule for relative vowel sounds

This rule helps predict when a vowel letter is pronounced with a relative vowel sound. The rule works for many words.

> ### The One Vowel Rule
>
> When there is only **one** vowel letter in a one-syllable word, it is usually pronounced with its relative vowel sound.
>
> For example, the letter -**a**- is pronounced /æ/ as in "sand" 91% of the time.*

 ## Practicing relative vowel sounds

Listen to the vowel sounds in these words. Repeat each word.

/æ/	/ɛ/	/ɪ/	/ɑ/	/ʌ/
has	bed	his	stop	up
cat	send	pin	shop	run
man	men	fill	Tom	lunch
plan	tell	dig	Bob	plum
sack	red	fish	dock	luck

 ## Contrasting alphabet vowel sounds and relative vowel sounds

Listen and repeat these pairs of words.

Alphabet vowel sound		Relative vowel sound	
aid	/eʸ/	add	/æ/
seat	/iʸ/	set	/ɛ/
mice	/ɑʸ/	miss	/ɪ/
soak	/oʷ/	sock	/ɑ/
cute	/uʷ/	cut	/ʌ/
paid	/eʸ/	pad	/æ/
cheese	/iʸ/	chess	/ɛ/
pike	/ɑʸ/	pick	/ɪ/
hope	/oʷ/	hop	/ɑ/
cube	/uʷ/	cub	/ʌ/

---

* For more information on this vowel rule, check Appendix C on page 144.

N ## Guessing the pronunciation of a word

1 Read the words below. You can use the vowel rules to guess how they should be pronounced. Mark the column that shows if the underlined letter is pronounced with its alphabet vowel sound or its relative vowel sound.

	Alphabet vowel sound	Relative vowel sound
1. r<u>o</u>ve	✔	
2. sp<u>a</u>n		✓
3. v<u>i</u>ce	✓	
4. m<u>oa</u>t	✓	
5. sl<u>ai</u>n	✓	
6. m<u>e</u>ld		✓
7. st<u>i</u>nt	✓	✓ ?
8. j<u>u</u>te	✓	

2 Listen to the words to see if you guessed the vowel sounds correctly.

 O ## Listening to contrasting vowels in sentences

Listen to each sentence and circle the word in **bold** that you hear.

1. Did you say ("hope") / "hop"?
2. How do you spell "lease" / ("less")?
3. What does "tape" / ("tap") mean?

4. I need a (pan) / pen.
5. Did you want (this) / these?
6. Do you like (chess) / cheese?

P ## Music of English ♪

1 Listen. Notice that there are two peaks of melody in the question. This is because two words are being compared. The vowels in the melody peaks must be said clearly.

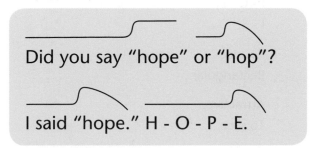

Did you say "hope" or "hop"?

I said "hope." H - O - P - E.

2 Listen again and repeat each sentence until you can say it easily. Learn it like a little song.

Q Pair work: Contrasting vowels

Student A: Say one word in the pair.
Student B: Ask which word was said.
Student A: Answer and spell the word you said.

Take turns saying the words. Do not always say the first word.

Example

Student A: Hop.
Student B: Did you say "hope" or "hop"?
Student A: I said "hop." H - O - P.

1. hope	hop		**4.** main	man		**7.** goat	got
2. bead	bed		**5.** bite	bit		**8.** pine	pin
3. cute	cut		**6.** lame	lamb		**9.** mean	men

R Pair work: Contrasting vowels in sentences

Student A: Ask question **a** or question **b**.
Student B: Say the answer.
Student A: If the answer is incorrect, repeat the question.

Take turns asking and answering the questions. Do not always ask question **a** first.

Example

Student A: What does "fad" mean?
Student B: A fashion for a short time.

1. a. What does "fade" mean?   To lose color.
  b. What does "fad" mean?   A fashion for a short time.

2. a. How do you spell "ice"?   I - C - E.
  b. How do you spell "is"?   I - S.

3. a. What shape is a bead?   Round.
  b. What shape is a bed?   Rectangular.

4. a. What does "cute" mean?   Attractive.
  b. What does "cut" mean?   To slice.

5. a. How do you spell "beast"?   B - E - A - S - T.
  b. How do you spell "best"?   B - E - S - T.

6. a. What's a pine?   A kind of tree.
  b. What's a pin?   Something with a sharp point.

S Check yourself: Alphabet vowel sounds and relative vowel sounds

1 Listen and repeat each sentence.

   1. Raisins are dried grapes.
   2. Prunes are dried plums.
   3. The pin is stuck in the seat.
   4. Clip this note to the box.

2 If possible, record yourself saying these sentences. Listen to your recording. Did you say the vowel sounds correctly?

T Dictation

1 Listen and write the sentences you hear.

   1. Did you say "teen" or "ten"?
   2. Is it a big pine
   3. I hope I can see it
   4. chocolate is not vegetable
   5. several elementry school open late

U Using the vowel symbols

/eʸ/	/iʸ/	/aʸ/	/oʷ/	/uʷ/
cake	tea	ice	cone	blue

/æ/	/ɛ/	/ɪ/	/ɑ/	/ʌ/
pan	ten	is	top	cut

In the tops of the pyramids, write the correct symbol for each peak vowel sound.

/ɪ/	....	....	....	....
peak vowel	peak vowel	peak vowel	peak vowel	peak vowel
1. is	2. ten	3. blue	4. cut	5. ice

Word Stress and Vowel Length

A Stressed syllables

1 Listen. The letter **-a-** appears three times in the word below. Notice how the vowel in the second syllable sounds different.

ban **a** na

2 Listen again. The vowel in the second syllable is longer. That is because the second syllable, *nan*, is the **stressed syllable** of the word. The vowel sound in the stressed syllable is the clearest and longest vowel in the word, the **peak vowel**. In this word, the peak vowel is the sound /æ/.

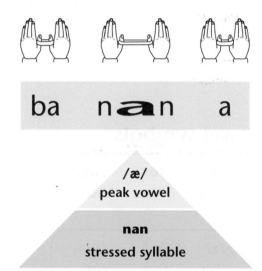

ba n **a** n a

/æ/
peak vowel

nan
stressed syllable

B Word stress and vowel length

The following rules will help you identify the stressed syllable in English words.

Rules for Stress and Vowel Length

1. In every English word of more than one syllable, one syllable is stressed the most.

2. The vowel sound in the stressed syllable is extra long. It is the peak vowel.

C Listening for vowel length

1 Listen. Notice how the vowel sound in the stressed syllable is extra long.

Ca nada	Jap a n	Chi na	Am e rica	E ngland

2 Listen. Underline the stressed syllable in each word.

<u>so</u>fa	at<u>tract</u>	solution	going
<u>oven</u>	<u>event</u>	ar<u>range</u>ment	<u>hor</u>rible
<u>ac</u>tion	ar<u>range</u>	pol<u>lu</u>tion	<u>ener</u>gy
<u>Lon</u>don	Bra<u>zil</u>	At<u>lan</u>ta	<u>Otta</u>wa
<u>Eng</u>land	Ber<u>lin</u>	Al<u>ber</u>ta	<u>Wash</u>ington

D Saying stressed syllables

Hmw

X

Listen and repeat these words. Pay attention to the length of the stressed syllable.

□□	□□
remain	mainly
amaze	soapy
arrive	reason
arrange	training
explain	sailing

α

E Saying words with more than two syllables

Listen and repeat these words. Be sure to lengthen the vowel in the stressed syllable.

□□□	□□□
attractive	principle = *rule or law*
atomic	politics
arrangement	sensitive
electric	minister *churchman/woman* & *attend—mind—take care*

minister to

α

F Pair work: Stress in acronyms

Each letter in an acronym* is pronounced separately, but the last letter usually gets the most stress.

1 Listen and notice how the last letter is stressed.

□□□	□□□	□□□
T V	B B C	U S A

---

* *Acronym*: a word made from the first letters of other words

2 Student A: Ask any question from the list.

Student B: Answer the question.

Take turns asking and answering the questions.

1. What does "TV" mean?   Television.
2. What does "UN" mean?   United Nations.
3. What does "DC" mean?   District of Columbia (Washington, D.C.).
4. What does "BC" mean?   British Columbia (Canada).
5. What does "USA" mean?   United States of America.
6. What does "BBC" mean?   British Broadcasting Company.
7. What does "CNN" mean?   Cable News Network.
8. What does "CBC" mean?   Canadian Broadcasting Corporation.
9. What does "UK" mean?   United Kingdom.
10. What does "IT" mean?   Information technology.

G The Two Vowel Rule with multi-syllable words

In Unit 2, you studied the Two Vowel Rule in one-syllable words. This same rule usually works for the stressed syllable of longer words.

The Two Vowel Rule for Multi-Syllable Words

If there are two vowel letters in the **stressed** syllable of a word:

1. The first vowel is pronounced with its alphabet sound.

2. The second vowel is silent.

For example, the letters **-ai-** are pronounced /eʸ/ as in "enter**tain**ment" 95% of the time.*

Listen and repeat these words. Be sure to use an alphabet vowel sound in the stressed syllable. The stressed syllable is in **bold**.

/eʸ/	/iʸ/	/aʸ/	/oʷ/	/uʷ/
cake	**tea**	**ice**	**cone**	**blue**
re**main**	re**peat**	a**live**	**soap**y	**Tues**day
e**rase**	de**lete**	in**side**	a**lone**	as**sume**
pa**rade**	re**treat**	pro**vide**	su**ppose**	intro**duce**
graceful	a**gree**ment	en**tire**ly	a**pproach**	con**fuse**
raisin	**rea**son	**price**less	**float**able	ex**cuse**

---

*For more information on this vowel rule, check Appendix C on page 144.

20 • Clear Speech

H The One Vowel Rule with multi-syllable words

The One Vowel Rule also works with many longer words.

> ### The One Vowel Rule for Multi-Syllable Words
>
> If there is only one vowel letter in the **stressed** syllable of a word, it is pronounced with its relative vowel sound.
>
> For example, the letter **-i-** is pronounced /ɪ/ as in "pre**scrip**tion" 93% of the time.

Listen and repeat these words. Be sure to use a relative vowel sound in the stressed syllable.

/æ/	/ɛ/	/ɪ/	/ɑ/	/ʌ/
pan	**ten**	**is**	**top**	**cut**
a**ttract**	**rel**ative	**fill**ing	**stopp**ing	**Sun**day
practice	**sent**ence	**print**er	**cop**y	be**gun**
ex**am**ple	su**ggest**	**prin**ciple	a**tom**ic	**thun**der
co**mmand**	e**lec**tric	**miss**ing	**tol**erance	**pun**ish
Saturday	ex**pen**sive	pre**dict**	**op**erate	a**bun**dant

I Music of English

1 Listen. Notice that there are two peaks in the answer. They are the stressed syllables and peak vowels of the important words.

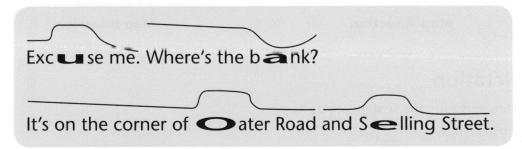

Exc**u**se me. Where's the b**a**nk?

It's on the corner of **O**ater Road and S**e**lling Street.

2 Listen again and repeat each sentence until you can say it easily. Learn it like a little song. Use two peaks for the answer.

J Pair work: Asking about locations

1 Student A: Look at Map A on page 23.
   Student B: Look at Map B on page 24.

2 Student A: Ask the location of a place in the list below the map.
   Student B: Tell your partner where the place is located. Make sure to use words only. Do not use your hands to point.
   Student A: Write the number of the place in the correct location on your map.

Take turns asking questions. When your maps are complete, check your answers. Did you write the numbers of the places in the correct locations?

Example

Student A: (Look at Map A.) Excuse me. Where's the bank?
Student B: (Look at Map B.) It's on the corner of Oater Road and Selling Street.
Student A: (Write the number "1" in the correct location on Map A.)

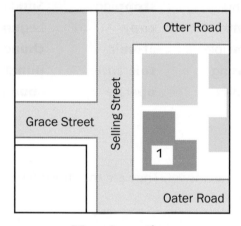

Map A section

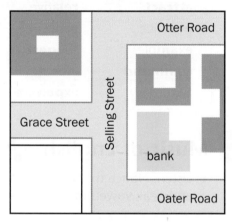

Map B section

K Dictation

Listen and write the sentences you hear.

1. Please remain seated.

2.

3.

4.

5.

Map A

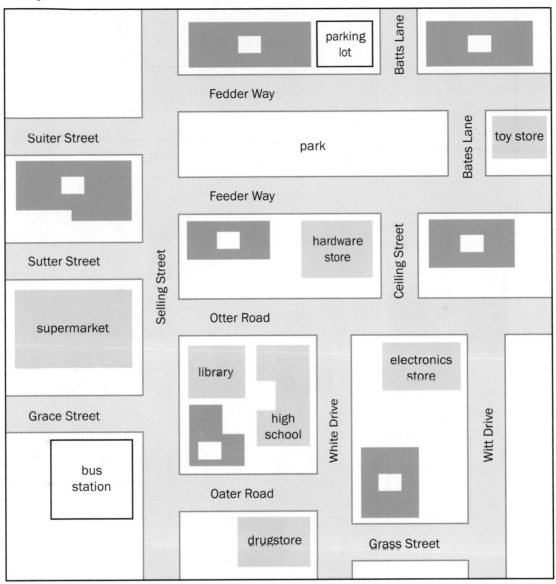

Places for Map A	
1. bank	5. bakery
2. hospital	6. preschool
3. restaurant	7. bookstore
4. post office	

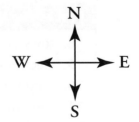

Map B

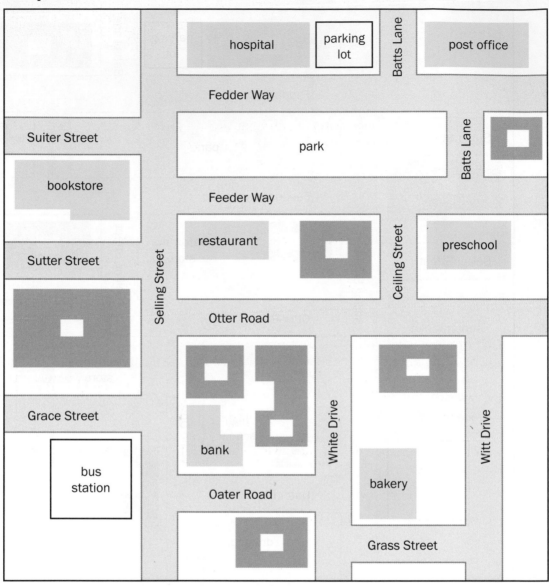

hospital

parking lot

post office

Batts Lane

Fedder Way

Suiter Street

park

Batts Lane

bookstore

Feeder Way

Sutter Street

restaurant

preschool

Ceiling Street

Selling Street

Grace Street

Otter Road

White Drive

Witt Drive

bank

bus station

bakery

Oater Road

Grass Street

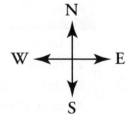

4 Word Stress and Vowel Clarity

🎧 A Clear vowels

You have been practicing saying the common vowel sounds of English clearly. When a syllable is stressed, the vowel sound in it is extra clear as well as extra long.

Listen. Which letter -a- in "banana" has a clear vowel sound?

Only the stressed -a- is said with a clear vowel sound and is extra long. This is the peak vowel in the word.

B Schwa, the unclear vowel

While stressed vowels must be clear, many other vowels are not said clearly. The other two vowels in "banana" are **reduced** to a very short, unclear sound. This sound is the reduced vowel, **schwa**. The reason many vowel sounds are reduced to schwa is to make a contrast with the clear peak vowel in the stressed syllable. Notice the following about the schwa vowel:

1. There is no letter for the schwa vowel sound, but the dictionary symbol for schwa is /ə/.

2. All of the vowel sounds in English can be reduced to schwa.

3. Schwa is the most common vowel sound in spoken English.

🎧 C The contrast between schwa and clear vowels

Listen. Notice the difference between schwa and the sound of a stressed vowel.

1. travel	tra vəl		6. Kansas	Ka nsəs
2. pilot	pi lət		7. Alaska	əl a skə
3. ticket	ti ckət		8. Nebraska	Nəbr a skə
4. pencil	pe ncəl		9. Canada	Ca nədə
5. advice	ədv i ce		10. America	əm e rəcə

e = repeat
ə
i = Cali

D Saying the contrast between schwa and clear vowels

1 Listen. Underline the vowel in the stressed syllable of each word.

1. l<u>i</u>sten
2. r<u>ea</u>son
3. all<u>ow</u>
4. att<u>e</u>nd
5. <u>A</u>frican
6. arr<u>a</u>nge
7. rec<u>o</u>rd
8. Americ<u>a</u>n
9. succ<u>e</u>ss
10. ann<u>ou</u>nce

2 Draw a slash through the vowels above that are reduced to a schwa sound.

lis~~e~~n

3 Practice saying the words. Make the vowel in the stressed syllable long and very clear but make the reduced vowels short and unclear.

E Pair work: Contrasting clear and reduced vowels

Student A: Say one word from each pair of words.
Student B: Say the other word in the pair.

Take turns saying the words. Be sure to make the reduced vowels short and unclear.

Example

Student A: Atom.
Student B: Tom.

1. Tom	T**o**m	atom	**a**təm	
2. at	**a**t	attend	ətt**e**nd	
3. man	m**a**n	woman	w**o**mən	
4. men	m**e**n	women	w**o**mən	
5. office	**o**ffəce	official	əff**i**cəl	
6. add	**a**dd	addition	ədd**i**tən	
7. added	**a**ddəd	additional	ədd**i**tənəl	
8. face	f**a**ce	surface	s**u**rfəce	

Identifying and saying schwa

1 Listen. Draw a slash through the vowels that are reduced to schwa.

	One reduced vowel	**Two reduced vowels**
relative o	problém photograph	adoptéd
	jacket overcast	application
	extra economics	collected
	dramatic	

2 Practice saying the words.

Vowel length and vowel clarity

In each word below there is one extra long, clear vowel and one vowel that is reduced to schwa. Each of these words also has one vowel that is not extra long, but it is not reduced to schwa, either.

1 Listen.

concentrate

c**○**ncəntrate

photograph

ph**○**təgraph

telephone

t**e**ləphone

2 Practice saying the words.

3 Read the rules below.

Stress Rules for Vowel Length and Vowel Clarity

1. The vowel in a stressed syllable is extra long and extra clear.

c**○**ncəntrate
↑

2. The vowel in an unstressed syllable is short and clear.

c**○**ncəntrate
↑

3. The vowel in a reduced syllable is very short and unclear (schwa).

c**○**ncəntrate
↑

Stressed vowels Long, clear	Unstressed vowels Short, clear	Reduced vowels Very short and unclear
a	a	ə
e	e	ə
i	i	ə
o	o	ə
u	u	ə
Very easy to hear	**Easy to hear**	Hard to hear

H Identifying stress in multi-syllable words

1 Listen. Underline the most stressed vowel in each word.

shuwa

1. attitude
2. institute
3. gratitude
4. military
5. secondary
6. reconsider
7. California
8. permission
9. constitution
10. understand
11. distribution
12. distributed

2 Practice saying the words.

I Limerick

1 Listen. The peak vowels in the stressed syllables in this limerick are long and clear. Most of the other vowels are reduced to schwa.

A **stu**dent was sent to Ta**co**ma
In**tend**ing to earn a di**plo**ma.
   He said, "With the **rain**,
   I don't want to re**main**.
I **think** I'd pre**fer** Okla**ho**ma "

Tacoma, Washington
Oklahoma
Washington, D.C.
(the U.S. capital)

2 Read the limerick out loud. Then whisper it. This will help you concentrate on the contrast between stressed and reduced vowels.

NOTE: Tacoma is an especially rainy city, and Oklahoma is an especially dry state.

J The vowel sounds in "can" and "can't"

Because it is important to make a contrast between "can" and "can't," in sentences, "can't" is usually said with the clear vowel sound /æ/, but the vowel sound in "can" is usually reduced to /ə/.

Listen to the following sentences. Notice the difference between the vowels in "can" and "can't."

We cæn't do it.

We cən do it.

 no more stronger

They said they cæn't be there

They said they cən be there.

You cæn't have mine.

You cən have mine.

K Pair work: "Can" and "can't"

Student A: Say sentence **a** or sentence **b**.

Student B: Say the matching response.

Take turns saying the sentences.

Example

Student A: I can't go.

Student B: That's too bad!

1. a. I can go.   Oh, good!
    b. I can't go.   That's too bad!

2. a. She can do it.   That's wonderful.
    b. She can't do it.   She should try harder.

3. a. Where can we go?   Any tourist destination.
    b. Where can't we go?   Into the military zone.

4. a. We can leave now.   Good, I'll get my coat.
    b. We can't leave now.   All right, we'll wait.

5. a. Can you lift this?   Of course.
    b. Can't you lift this?   No, I can't.

6. a. Why can you do that?   Because I have permission.
    b. Why can't you do that? Because I don't know how.

Music of English

1 Listen. Notice which vowel is extra long and extra clear in each sentence. This is the peak vowel in the stressed syllable.

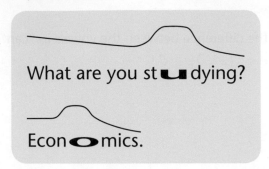

2 Listen again and repeat each sentence until you can say it easily.

M Check yourself: Stressed syllables

1 Listen to the dialogue. Notice which vowel is extra long and extra clear in each sentence. Circle the stressed syllable in the underlined words.

Students

A: What are you studying?

B: Economics. What about you?

A: Photography.

B: Then you must take good photographs.

A: And you must be good with money!

2 Practice saying the dialogue, alone or with another student.

3 If possible, record yourself saying the dialogue. Listen to your recording. Did you make the stressed vowels extra long and extra clear?

N Dictation

Listen and write the sentences you hear.

1. My hobby is painting.
2. ....
3. ....
4. ....
5. ....

VOWEL WORK

 ## The letters -y- and -w- as vowel sounds

In many words, the letters **-y-** and **-w-** are pronounced as vowel sounds.

1 Sometimes the letter **-y-** sounds like the alphabet vowel sound /iʸ/ in "tea" or the alphabet vowel sound /aʸ/ in "ice."

Listen and repeat these words.

tea /iʸ/			**ice** /aʸ/	
funny	happy		why	apply
pretty	lazy		sky	type
city	comedy		my	reply
electricity	studying		fly	shy
history	photography		cry	supply

2 When the letter **-y-** follows the letter **-a-** in a word, it often acts like a second vowel, so the letter **-a-** sounds like the vowel sound in "cake." For words like this, the Two Vowel Rule works about 93% of the time.

Listen and repeat these words.

cake /eʸ/	
say	today
pays	astray
stayed	dismay
may	player
way	always

3 When the letter **-y-** follows the letter **-e-** in the last syllable of a word, the letter **-e-** often has the vowel sound of "tea." For words like this, the Two Vowel Rule works about 91% of the time.

Listen and repeat these words.

tea /iʸ/	
donkey	hockey
honey	monkeys
money	valley
alley	chimney

4 When the letter **-w-** follows the letter **-o-** in a word, it often acts like a second vowel, so the letter **-o-** sounds like the vowel sound in "cone." The Two Vowel Rule works for these words about 53% of the time.

Listen and repeat these words.

cone /oʷ/

show	knowing
slow	growing
follow	snow
throw	own
below	narrow

5 Practice saying these sentences.

1. I want to apply for the job, but I can't type.
2. Give her the money so she can pay.
3. That was a very funny show.

Linking vowels with an off-glide 🔗

English speakers link words together in natural speech. The final sound in one word often connects with the first sound in the next word, with no pause between the words.

For example, when the words "we agree" are said together, it sounds like one word, "weagree."

When the vowel sounds /iʸ/, /aʸ/, or /eʸ/ link with a following vowel, the vowel sounds are connected by the off-glide /ʸ/.

1 Listen and notice how these words are linked by an off-glide.

1. We agree.   Weʸagree.

2. I often say a lot.   Iʸoften sayʸa lot.

2 Say these words together at least two times. Continue to say the final sound of the first word until you start to say the next word.

1. say it	sayʸit		4. pay us	payʸus
2. I am	Iʸam		5. cry out	cryʸout
3. stay away	stayʸaway		6. see everything	seeʸeverything

3 Say the following sentences, linking with the off-glide /ʸ/.

1. Primary education is very important.
2. We always try to see everything.
3. They all want to say it.

 Using vowel symbols

The peak vowel is the stressed vowel of the most important word in a sentence or thought group. That is why this vowel must be clear. Vowel sound symbols help you pay attention to the clarity of the vowel.

/æ/	/ɛ/	/ɪ/	/ɑ/	/ʌ/
panic	**ten**sion	**wish**ful	**top**ic	**butt**er

/eʸ/	/iʸ/	/aʸ/	/oʷ/	/uʷ/
a**fraid**	**sea**son	a**rrive**	a**pproach**	a**ccuse**

Write the correct stressed syllable in the second level of the pyramid and the correct vowel sound symbol in the top level of the pyramid for these words.

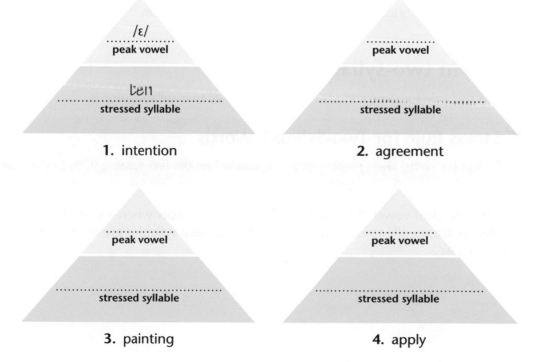

1. intention

2. agreement

3. painting

4. apply

Word Stress Patterns

A Listening to stress patterns

Every English word has a stress pattern. Because English listeners recognize a word by the stress, using the correct pattern is even more important than using the correct sounds.

Listen to the following words and notice their stress patterns.

President   **Prime Min**ister

If you say a word using its correct stress pattern, it is easier for other people to understand you, even if you do not get every sound exactly right.

B Review: Identifying stressed syllables

Listen. Underline the stressed syllable in each word. Remember that the vowel in the stressed syllable is extra long and extra clear.

hamburger	extremely	refrigerate	electric
cookies	accurate	refrigerator	electrical
pizza	dinner	refrigeration	electrification

C Stress in two-syllable words

1 Read this rule for predicting the stress pattern of two-syllable words.

> ### Stress Rule for Two-Syllable Words
>
> Except for verbs, two-syllable words are stressed on the first syllable 90% of the time.

NOTE: The clear vowel of the first syllable helps you know when a word begins. First syllables are usually stressed syllables, and unstressed syllables are often said with a schwa, /ə/.

2 Listen and repeat these two-syllable words.

☐■

lemon	l**e**mən
jacket	j**a**ckət
older	**o**ldər
winter	w**i**ntər

☐■

rocket	r**o**ckət
open	**o**pən
student	st**u**dənt
April	**A**prəl

3 Listen and repeat these two-syllable names.

☐■

Susan	S**u**sən
Jacob	J**a**cəb
Ethan	**E**thən
Justin	J**u**stən

☐■

Emma	**E**mmə
Kevin	K**e**vən
Michael	M**i**chəl
Anna	**A**nnə

4 Can you think of other two-syllable English names that have the same stress pattern?

🎧 **D** # Stress in words that end in *-tion*, *-sion*, and *-cian*

The following words all end in the letters **-tion**, **-sion**, or **-cian**. All of these endings are pronounced /ʃən/.

1 Listen to the stress pattern of these words. Underline the stressed syllable.

☐☐☐

reduction
musician
correction
permission
instruction

☐☐☐☐

electrician
complication
occupation
politician
regulation

☐☐☐☐☐

participation
examination
administration
contamination
organization

2 Say the words while paying attention to the stress pattern.

except: television

3 Here is a useful rule for stress in words that end in **-tion, -sion,** or **-cian.**

> ## Stress Rule for the /ʃən/ Ending
>
> For words that end in **-tion, -sion,** or **-cian,** the stressed syllable comes just before the **-tion, -sion,** or **-cian** ending.

4 Use the rule above to find the stressed syllable in the words below. Underline the stressed syllable and then say the words.

prediction	magician	education	commission
vacation	election	impression	aggravation

E Stress in words that end in *-ic* and *-ical*

1 Listen. Which syllable is stressed in the following words?

Atlantic	robotic	comic	terrific	automatic
majestic	narcotic	economic	Pacific	photographic
domestic	statistic	dramatic	diplomatic	democratic

2 Write a stress rule for words that end in **-ic.** Check your answer on page 43.

> ## Stress Rule for the *-ic* Ending
>
> ....
>
> ....

3 Listen. Which syllable is stressed in the following list of words?

economical	comical
technological	political
surgical	chemical

4 Write a rule for stress in words that end in **-ical.** Check your answer on page 43.

> ## Stress Rule for the *-ical* Ending
>
> ....
>
> ....

Pronouncing two clear vowels together

Sometimes when two vowels are next to each other in a word, they are actually separate syllables. In that case, both vowels are clear.

Notice the dot between the vowels. This dot separates the syllables. Usually, the second clear vowel has the stress, so it is longer.

Listen and repeat these words. The stressed syllable is in **bold**.

biology	bi•**o**l•o•gy	piano	pi•**a**n•o	reaction	re•**a**c•tion
re**a**lity		ge**o**graphy		ge**o**logy	
cre**ate**		recre**a**tion		associ**a**tion	

 ## Stress in two-syllable nouns and verbs

The following two-syllable words have a noun form and a verb form.

1 Listen and underline the stressed syllables. Which syllable is stressed for the nouns? Which syllable is stressed for the verbs?

Noun		Verb	
1. <u>re</u>cord	**re**•cərd	re<u>cord</u>	rəc•**o**rd
2. <u>ob</u>ject		ob<u>ject</u>	
3. <u>per</u>mit		per<u>mit</u>	
4. <u>sus</u>pect		sus<u>pect</u>	
5. <u>im</u>port		im<u>port</u>	
6. <u>re</u>bel		re<u>bel</u>	
7. <u>pre</u>sent		pre<u>sent</u>	
8. <u>con</u>flict		con<u>flict</u>	
9. <u>in</u>sult		in<u>sult</u>	

2 Practice saying the noun and verb form of each word.

3 Read this rule.

> ### Stress Rule for Two-Syllable Verbs
>
> When a two-syllable word can be used as either a noun or a verb, the verb form is usually stressed on the second syllable.

H Which word do you hear?

Listen. Circle the word you hear. The stressed syllable is in **bold**.

Noun	Verb
1. **con**tract	(con**tract**)
2. **ex**port	ex**port**
3. **pro**gress	pro**gress**
4. **re**ject	re**ject**
5. **trans**port	trans**port**
6. **pre**sent	pre**sent**
7. **con**flict	con**flict**
8. **con**vert	con**vert**

disagreement
fight
difference of opinion

to fight, to come into opposition

transform, change

I Stress in two-word verbs

Some verbs are made up of two words. These two-word verbs are commonly stressed on the second syllable.

Listen to the stress pattern for these nouns and two-word verbs.

Noun	Verb
1. a **set**up (an arrangement)	set **up** (to arrange)
2. a **hold**up (a robbery)	hold **up** (to rob something or someone)
3. a **look**out (a person who watches)	look **out** (to be careful)
4. a **try**out (a test, an audition)	try **out** (to test something or someone)
5. a **check**out (a place to pay a bill)	check **out** (to pay a bill and leave)
6. a **turn**off (something you do not like)	turn **off** (to displease)
7. a **cut**back (less of something)	cut **back** (to use less of something)
8. a **start**up (a new company)	start **up** (to begin)

cutdown = (next to item 7)

you need to cut back coffee

you have to cutdown on beer drinking

 ## Music of English

1 Listen. Notice the change in the stressed syllables. One word is a verb and the other is a noun.

Do they susp**e**ct him?

Y**e**s, he's a s**u**spect.

2 Listen again and repeat each sentence until you can say it easily.

K Pair work: Noun or verb?

Student A: Say the noun (**a**) or the verb (**b**) in the first column.
Student B: Say the sentence that contains the noun or verb that your partner said.

NOTE: The words and sentences continue on the next page.

Examples

Student A: **Sus**pect.
Student B: He's a **sus**pect.
Student A: Ob**ject**.
Student B: We ob**ject** to that!

1. a. **sus**pect   He's a **sus**pect.
    b. sus**pect**   Do they sus**pect** him of the crime?

2. a. **ob**ject   What's this little **ob**ject?
    b. ob**ject**   We ob**ject** to that plan!

3. a. **re**cord   Our team has the **re**cord for most wins.
    b. re**cord**   We re**cord** our team's wins on the Internet.

4. a. **pre**sent   We gave her a **pre**sent.
    b. pre**sent**   They plan to pre**sent** her with an award.

5. a. **con**flict   The two leaders had a terrible **con**flict.
    b. con**flict**   His views con**flict** with mine.

6. a. **con**tract   They agreed to sign a **con**tract.
    b. con**tract**   Cold air makes metal con**tract**.

7. a. **check**out	We need to pay at the **check**out counter.	
b. check **out**	We need to check **out** of the hotel.	
8. a. **cut**back	There might be a **cut**back in our pay.	
b. cut **back**	The company cut **back** on the number of workers.	

Stress in compound nouns

English often combines two nouns to make a new word, called a **compound noun**. For example, the words "house" and "boat" can be combined to form a new noun.

1 Listen.

house + boat = **house**boat

> ### Stress Rule for Compound Nouns
> Compound nouns are pronounced as a single word, with the stress on the first part.

2 Practice saying these compound nouns.

bathroom	**key**board	**post** office
raincoat	**note**book	**key** chain
bookstore	**base**ball	**cof**fee pot
airline	**book**mark	**hot** dog

NOTE: Sometimes compound nouns are written as one word, and sometimes they are written as two words. Check your dictionary.

Check yourself: Dialogue

1 Look at the underlined words in the dialogue on the next page. Their stressed syllables are in **bold**.

2 Read the dialogue out loud, alone, or with a partner. Be sure to make the vowels in the stressed syllables extra long and extra clear.

NOTE: For most people, "business" has two syllables. The letter **-u-** in the first syllable has the relative vowel sound /ɪ/ as in "his" – /bɪz•nəs/. For most people, "interesting" has three syllables – /ɪn•trəs•tɪŋ/.

Conversation on a Train

(Two commuters are talking while on their way to work in the city.)

Commuter 1:   What **bus**iness are you in?

Commuter 2:   Pho**to**graphy.

Commuter 1:   Oh, yeah? **In**teresting. Is there a lot of **mon**ey in it?

Commuter 2:   Well, you have to look **out** for ex**pen**ses. They can cre**ate** a real **prob**lem.

Commuter 1:   Really? And how much **mon**ey do you need to set **up** a **bus**iness like that?

Commuter 2:   Oh, a lot! The **set**up is ex**pen**sive – com**pu**ters, photo**graph**ic e**quip**ment. Lots of stuff.

Commuter 1:   I see. Well, maybe I'll just stick to my **pres**ent occu**pa**tion.

3 If possible, record yourself saying the dialogue. Listen to your recording. Did you lengthen the stressed syllables?

VOWEL WORK

 ## The spelling *-ow-* pronounced /uʷ/ as in "cow"

As you learned in Unit 4, the letters **-ow-** are pronounced with the sound /oʷ/, as in "know" and "show," about 53% of the time. However, **-ow-** is also sometimes pronounced with a different vowel sound, /aʷ/ as in "cow."

1 Listen and repeat these words.

cow /aʷ/	
now	brown
how	crowd
down	allow
town	towel
gown	powder

2 Practice saying these sentences.

 1. This town is very crowded.

 2. Please hand me the brown towel.

 3. Now she understands how to do it.

🎧 O The spelling -*ew*- pronounced /uʷ/ as in "new"

Syllables spelled with -**ew**- are pronounced /uʷ/ as in "new" about 89% of the time. This is the same sound as the vowel in "blue."

1 Listen and repeat these words.

> **blue** /uʷ/

knew	new
chew	crew
grew	dew
stew	jewel
flew	sewage

2 Practice saying these sentences.

NOTE: The vowel sound in "few" is /yuʷ/ as in "cube."

 1. The baby is trying to chew with her new teeth.

 2. The crew knew how to fly the plane, but they refused.

 3. Our puppy grew very fast in a few weeks.

🎧 P Linking vowels with an off-glide 🔗

When the vowel sounds /oʷ/, /aʷ/, or /uʷ/ link with a following vowel, the sounds are connected by the off-glide /ʷ/.

1 Listen and notice how these words are linked by an off-glide.

 1. Please go͜ on.   Please goʷon .

 2. How͜ about it?   Howʷabout it?

 3. I knew͜ it.   I knewʷit .

2 Say these words together at least two times. Continue to say the final sound of the first word until you start to say the next word.

1. new edition   new͜ʷedition   4. how old   how͜ʷold

2. a few eggs   few͜ʷeggs   5. throw it   throw͜ʷit

3. so often   so͜ʷoften   6. no ice   no͜ʷice

3 Say these sentences, linking with the off-glide /ʷ/.

1. I know all the songs, so I can lead the singing.
2. How old is the new edition?
3. We flew over the blue ocean.
4. There's no snow anywhere.

 Dictation

Listen and write the sentences you hear.

1. <u>He knows how to play the piano.</u> ....

2. ....

3. ....

4. ....

5. ....

Answers to Task E (page 36)

2 Stress Rule for the -ic Ending:
For words that end in **-ic**, the stressed syllable comes just before the **-ic** ending.

4 Stress Rule for the -ical Ending:
For words that end in **-ical**, the stressed syllable comes just before the **-ical** ending.

6 | Sentence Focus: Emphasizing Content Words

🎧 A Contrast

1 Compare the two pictures below. In the picture on the left, the butterfly is hard to see because it is the same color as the things around it. The butterfly on the right is lighter than everything else around it. This contrast between light and dark makes the butterfly easier to notice.

2 This is the same kind of contrast English speakers use to stress a syllable and its peak vowel in important words. This contrast helps emphasize important words so that they are easy for a listener to notice.

Listen. One word in the sentence below is emphasized and the other words are de-emphasized. This is **_contrast_**.

How do you spell "easy"?

🎧 B Focus words

In each thought group (a short sentence, clause, or phrase), there is only one most important word. This word is the **_focus word_**. You can help your listeners notice the focus word by giving it extra emphasis. To make a strong contrast, the stressed vowel in the focus word must be pronounced with extra clarity.

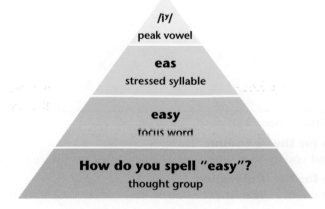

/iʸ/
peak vowel

eas
stressed syllable

easy
focus word

How do you spell "easy"?
thought group

Focus Rule 1

There is a pitch change on the vowel of the stressed syllable of the focus word. The pitch change can be up or down, but it must be a change.

Listen.

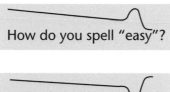

How do you spell "easy"?

How do you spell "easy"?

 C **Music of English**

1 Listen. Notice how the stressed syllable of the focus word in each sentence has a pitch change. This change in melody makes clear which word is important.

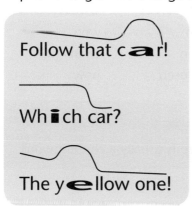

Follow that c**a**r!

Wh**i**ch car?

The y**e**llow one!

2 Listen again and repeat each sentence until you can say it easily. Use the same melody to emphasize the important words.

 D **Finding the focus word**

Listen. Underline the focus word that the speaker emphasizes in each sentence.

1. We'll be arriving <u>tomorrow</u>.
2. You look <u>great.</u>
3. She lives in <u>Toronto</u> now.

4. Is the baby <u>walking</u> yet?
5. Where are we <u>going</u>?
6. I'm always <u>hungry</u>.

E Music of English 🎵

1 Listen. Notice how the focus words are emphasized. The stressed syllable of each focus word has both a change in pitch and a long, clear vowel.

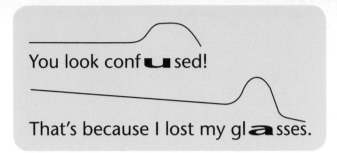

You look conf**u**sed!

That's because I lost my gl**a**sses.

2 Listen again and repeat each sentence until you can say it easily.

F Focus and content words

The words that were emphasized in the sentences you just learned are ***content words***. Here are some examples of content words:

Nouns	Main verbs	Adverbs	Adjectives	Question words
cat	run	suddenly	fresh	who
bus	read	carefully	green	what
glasses	eat	slowly	confused	how

Focus Rule 2

The focus word in a short sentence or thought group is usually a content word.

G Content word game

Divide into teams. In five minutes write as many content words as you can think of for each category.

Nouns	Main verbs	Adverbs	Adjectives	Question words
baby	walk	quickly	green	when
cat	swim	slowly	fresh	what
bus	write	gracefully	lovely	who
glasses	read	kindly	kind	where
		totaly	ugly	
			friendly	

H Emphasizing the focus word

The focus words in these sentences are underlined. Each of these focus words is a different category of content word.

1 Listen to the sentences and hear how the focus words are emphasized.

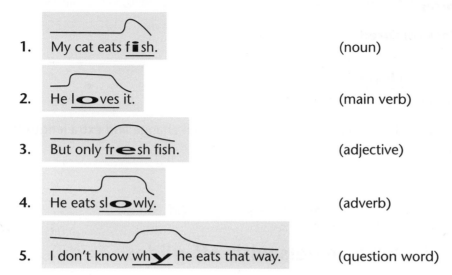

1. My cat eats f**i**sh.   (noun)

2. He l**o**ves it.   (main verb)

3. But only fr**e**sh fish.   (adjective)

4. He eats sl**o**wly.   (adverb)

5. I don't know wh**y** he eats that way.   (question word)

2 Practice saying the sentences. Be sure to emphasize the focus word.

I Adding the focus word

1 Add a content word to each sentence. The content word you add will be the focus word.

1. I can't .... (main verb)

2. He's riding a .... (noun)

3. The baby is .... (main verb)

4. Please hand me the .... (noun)

5. The food is much too .... (adjective)

6. I'm not sure .... she's going. (question word)

7. He drives .... (adverb)

2 Practice saying the sentences. Emphasize the focus words.

✳✳the last word is usually focus word.
(when it's new information.)

J Pair work: Dialogue

1 Listen to the dialogue. The underlined content word in each sentence is the focus word. The stressed syllable is in **bold**. Notice that there are two focus words in the last sentence because it has two thought groups.

Lost Glasses

A: You look con**fused**.

B: That's because I lost my **gla**sses!

A: Where'd you **leave** them?

B: If I **knew** that, I could **find** them!

2 Practice saying the dialogue. Be sure to add a pitch change and extra length to the stressed syllable of each focus word.

VOWEL WORK

K Review: Linking vowels with off-glides

1 Some of the words in the following stories link together with an off-glide. Write a small ʸ or a small ʷ between the words to show which off-glide links them together.

2 Read the stories below out loud, linking with the appropriate off-glide.

At the Beach

Weʸ often go to the beach on the weekend. We always go by car, because it's fastest. My roommate will try anything. He loves to surf, but he isn't a great surfer. He always falls off the surfboard. "What's the answer?" he asked me. "I hate to say it, but I think you should find another sport," I said.

Jokes Between Friends

Sometimes I goʷ over to my friend's house. The first thing she says when we meet is "How are you?" But if I really tell her how I am, she doesn't listen. This happens so often that I decided to answer "fine" every time.

But then one day I said, "You never listen." So she apologized and said, "From now on I'll do better." Then she asked, "How are you?" and I said, "Terrible!" She knew I was joking, so she said, "That's great! See how I'm listening to everything you say?"

Dictation

Listen and write the sentences you hear.

when

1. We all want the best solution.
2. ....
3. ....
4. ....
5. ....

M Review

Your English listeners will understand you more easily if you emphasize the focus word and its stressed syllable, and if you make the peak vowel clear.

Fill in the focus word and the stressed syllable of the thought group in the pyramid. Use the peak vowel sound at the top of the pyramid to help you find the focus word and stressed syllable.

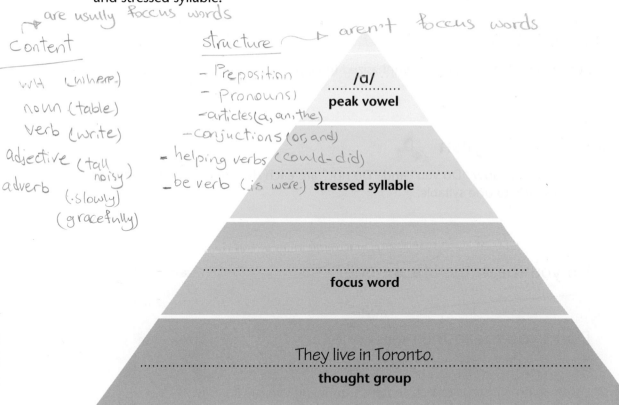

→ are usully foccus words

Content ___

wld (where)
noun (table)
verb (write)
Adjective (tall noisy)
adverb (.slowly)
(gracefully)

structure → aren't foccus words

- Preposition
- Pronouns)
- articles (a, an, the)
- conjuctions (or, and)
= helping verbs (could - did)
- be verb (is were)

/a/
peak vowel

stressed syllable

focus word

They live in Toronto.
thought group

Sentence Focus: De-emphasizing Structure Words

A Focus and structure words

Most words that are not content words are **structure words**. Structure words are short words like "the" and "to." These words do not carry as much information as content words. The focus word in a sentence is usually *not* a structure word.

Here are some examples of structure words:

Pronouns	Prepositions	Articles*	Conjunctions	Auxiliary verbs	"to be" verbs
she	of	a	and	can	is
him	to	an	but	have	was
you	at	the	yet	do	were

Focus Rule 3

Structure words are usually de-emphasized to help make a contrast with the focus word.

B Music of English

1 Listen. Notice how "Do you" and "Do not" are each de-emphasized by reducing their sounds to one syllable.

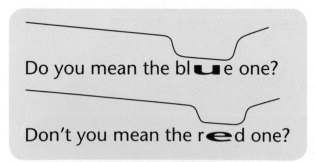

Do you mean the bl**u**e one?

Don't you mean the r**e**d one?

2 Listen again and repeat each sentence until you can say it easily.

---

* These are the only articles in English.

De-emphasizing structure words: Contractions

There are different ways to de-emphasize a structure word in English. One way is by **contraction**.

"To contract" means to make smaller. Contraction helps make structure words like "do" and "not" less noticeable, and this makes the focus words more noticeable.

1 Notice how the following structure words are contracted.

you + have	=	you've
he + would	=	he'd
can + not	=	can't
I + will	=	I'll

NOTE: Because contractions are so common in spoken English, practice saying them will help you hear and understand them more easily.

2 Listen to the difference between some common contractions and their full forms. Repeat the words and tap for each syllable.

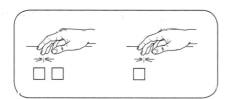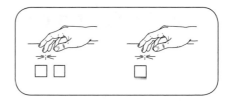

Full form	**Contraction**	**Full form**	**Contraction**
I am	I'm	he has	he's
do not	don't	I will	I'll
they have	they've	I have	I've
that is	that's	we have	we've
I would	I'd	will not	won't
I had	I'd	do you	d'you

D Group work: Saying contractions

Divide into two groups.

Group A: Say the first word of the full form.
Group B: Say the second word of the full form.
Both groups: Say the contraction together.

Example

Group A: She.
Group B: Is.
Both groups: She's.

Full form	Contraction
1. she is	she's
2. can not	can't
3. I have	I've
4. why have	why've
5. he has	he's
6. who is	who's
7. where did	where'd
8. we are	we're
9. they are	they're
10. he had	he'd

E Pair work: Saying contractions in sentences

Student A: Say sentence **a** or sentence **b** with the contraction.
Student B: Say the correct full form.

Example

Student A: They'd already gone.
Student B: They had.

Contraction	Full form
1. a. They've already gone.	they have
b. They'd already gone.	they had
2. a. Where'd you put that?	where did
b. Where'll you put that?	where will

3. a. We're shut down completely.   we are
   b. We'd shut down completely.   we had

4. a. We'd be pleased to help.   we would
   b. We'll be pleased to help.   we will

5. a. They'll cut the bread.   they will
   b. They've cut the bread.   they have

6. a. What've you put in the soup?   what have
   b. What'll you put in the soup?   what will

7. a. Where'd everybody go?   where did
   b. Where'll everybody go?   where will

8. a. I've run in that race.   I have
   b. I'll run in that race.   I will

F Saying common expressions with contractions

Listen and repeat these common friendly greetings and expressions. Each one contains a contraction.

1. What's new?
2. How're you doing?
3. How's it going?
4. How've you been?

5. What's up?
6. What'll you have? (to eat or drink)
7. It's great to see you!
8. I don't believe it!

G Linking in common expressions

Some of the words in these common expressions link together. For example, the final /z/ sound in "how's" connects with the vowel sound in "it" so that the two words sound like one word, "howzit."

1 Listen and notice how some of the words in these expressions link together.

1. How's it going? | Howzit | going?

2. What's up? | Whatsup | ?

3. I don't believe it!   I don't | believit | !

2 Practice saying these expressions again.

H De-emphasizing structure words: Reductions

Some structure words in English are de-emphasized by reducing the vowel in the structure word to schwa, /ə/. Reducing structure words in this way makes the more important words easier to notice. Words like "a," "an," and "or" that begin with a vowel sound are often linked to the final sound of the word that comes before them.

He takes a bus to work.   He takesə bus tə work.

1 Listen to the way the vowels in many of these structure words are reduced to schwa. Also notice how the structure words "a," "an," and "or" link to the word that comes before them.

1. He takes a bus to work.   He takesə bus tə work.

2. They wrote a letter to the president.   They wroteə letter tə thə president.

3. I left an umbrella in your car.   I leftən umbrella in yər car.

4. She runs or swims every day.   She runsər swims every day.

2 Practice saying the sentences.

 I De-emphasizing structure words: Reduced "and"

The structure word "and" is de-emphasized by reducing it to /ən/. The vowel sound is reduced to schwa, and the letter **-d-** is silent. The schwa sound in "and" is also linked to the final sound of the word that comes before it.

When "and" is reduced, the word before it and the word after it are easier to notice.

cream and sugar   creamən sugar

Listen to the way "and" is reduced and linked to the word that comes before it.

cream and sugar   creamən sugar

men and women   menən women

rock and roll   rockən roll

Linking with reduced "and"

Practice saying these phrases with reduced "and." Remember to link the reduced "and" to the word that comes before it.

cats and dogs   knives and forks

sandwich and coffee   bread and butter

big and little   hamburgers and fries

rich and famous   salt and pepper

tables and chairs   boys and girls

 K **De-emphasizing structure words: Silent letter -*h*-**

Structure words that begin with the letter -**h**-, like "he" and "her," are usually reduced by making the -**h**- silent. The vowel sound after the silent -**h**- links with the word that comes before it. For example, the question "Is he?" usually sounds like "Izzy?"

Is he?

1 Listen. Notice how the beginning -**h**- in these words is silent. Also notice how the consonant at the end of the first word links to the vowel of the structure word because the -**h**- is silent.

1. What's her name?   Whatser   name?

2. Call him.   Callim   .

3. I can't reach her.   I can't   reacher   .

4. Matt lost his jacket.   Matt   lostiz   jacket.

5. Will he be there?   Wille   be there?

6. Has anyone seen him?   Has anyone   seenim   ?

NOTE: When a structure word beginning in -**h**- is the first word in a sentence, the -**h**- is not silent. For example, the -**h**- is not silent in the sentence "He's going later."

2 Practice saying the sentences.

L Pair work: Linking over the silent letter -*h*- ⌒⌒⌒

1 Read the following sentences and draw an *X* through each -**h**- that should be silent.

2 Draw linking marks to connect the vowel after the silent -**h**- to the word that comes before it.

3 Student A: Say sentence **a** or sentence **b**.

Student B: Say the matching response.

Take turns choosing a sentence to say.

Example

Student A: Did he go?
Student B: No, he didn't.

1. a. Did H̶e go?   No, H̶e didn't.
    b. Did she go?   Yes, she did.

2. a. Is her work good?   Yes, she does well.
    b. Is his work good?   Yes, he does a great job.

3. a. Give him a call.   I don't know his number.
    b. Give me a call.   OK, what's your number?

4. a. Did you take her pen? No, it's mine.
    b. Did you take your pen? No, I forgot.

5. a. Is this his apartment? No, he lives upstairs.
    b. Is this Sue's apartment? No, she lives downstairs.

6. a. Is he busy?   No, he isn't.
    b. Is she busy?   Yes, she is.

∩M Pair work: Dialogue

1 Read the dialogue on the next page. Cross out each silent -**h**-.

2 Listen to the dialogue to see if you crossed out every silent -**h**-.

The Missing Singer

Stage Manager:	Where's our singer?
Assistant:	I think ~~H~~e's practicing, sir.
Stage Manager:	But we need him on stage now!
Assistant:	Well, you know how nervous he gets.
Stage Manager:	Did you tell him the concert's about to start?
Assistant:	He's practicing just as fast as he can.

3 Practice the dialogue with a partner. Be sure to link over each silent **-h-**.

∩N Limerick

1 Listen. Find the three structure words with a silent **-h-** in the following limerick.

A Train Ride

A singer once went to Vancouver,

Thinking the move would improve her.

But the trip was so long,

And her voice grew so strong,

At Toronto they had to remove her.

2 Practice saying the limerick and be sure to link over each silent **-h-**.

∩O Dictation

Listen and write the sentences you hear.

1. *Did he give her the book?* ....

2. ....

3. ....

4. ....

5. ....

VOWEL WORK

 P ## The spelling -*igh*- pronounced /aʸ/ as in "night"

The spelling -**igh**- is pronounced /aʸ/ 100% of the time. This is the same sound as the vowel in "ice."

1 Listen and repeat these words.

ice /aʸ/

tight	sigh
night	high
sight	bright
right	tonight
thigh	mighty

2 Practice saying these sentences.

1. Make a right at the next light.
2. Tonight the sky will be bright with stars.
3. How high is the plane flying?

 Q ## The spelling -*oo*- pronounced /uʷ/ as in "moon"

The spelling -**oo**- is pronounced /uʷ/ about 88% of the time. This is the same sound as the vowel in "blue."

1 Listen and repeat these words.

blue /uʷ/

too	tool
noon	balloon
moon	foolish
cool	kangaroo
choose	boomerang

2 Practice saying these sentences.

1. Australia has kangaroos and boomerangs, too.
2. Which room did you choose?
3. I hope it's cooler this afternoon.

8 | Choosing the Focus Word

 A ## Focus at the beginning of a conversation

This rule will help you decide which word to emphasize when beginning a conversation.

> ### Focus Rule 4
> At the beginning of a conversation, the focus word is usually the last content word in a thought group (a short sentence, clause, or phrase).

1 Listen to the following examples.

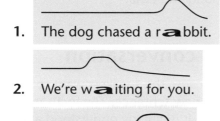

1. The dog chased a r**a**bbit.

2. We're w**a**iting for you.

3. What are you d**o**ing?

2 Listen. Hum the melody of each sentence with the pitch pattern shown. (Humming is singing with your mouth closed.)

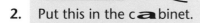

1. Here's a p**a**ckage for you.

2. Put this in the c**a**binet.

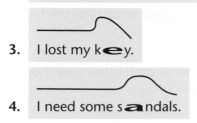

3. I lost my k**e**y.

4. I need some s**a**ndals.

3 Practice saying the sentences. Be sure to make the vowel in the stressed syllable of the focus word extra long and clear. Also be sure to raise or lower the pitch of your voice on the focus word.

B Finding the focus word

1 Underline the final content word in each of the following sentences. Circle the stressed syllable in this word.

1. There's no elec(tri)city.
2. We need a photograph.
3. This is my sister.
4. Can I help you?
5. He doesn't under(stand) it.
6. Where did you go?
7. Open the window for them.
8. Please re(cord) this for me.

2 Practice saying the sentences with a pitch change on the stressed syllable. Be sure to make the vowel in the stressed syllable extra long and clear.

C Focus after the beginning of a conversation

After a conversation begins, the focus changes because the speakers want to call attention to the **new thought** introduced in each new sentence. The focus word of the sentence that came before is now an **old thought**. It is already understood and does not need emphasis.

> ### Focus Rule 5
>
> After a conversation begins, any word can become a new thought (the new focus of information).

1 Listen to this dialogue. Notice which word is the focus word in each sentence.

The Lost Hat

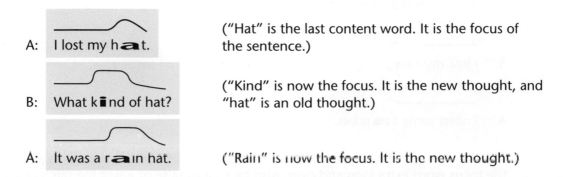

A: I lost my h**a**t.

("Hat" is the last content word. It is the focus of the sentence.)

B: What k**i**nd of hat?

("Kind" is now the focus. It is the new thought, and "hat" is an old thought.)

A: It was a r**a**in hat.

("Rain" is now the focus. It is the new thought.)

B: What c⬭lor rain hat?

A: It was wh◾te. White pl⬭stic.

B: Hmmm. There was a white hat in the c⬭r.

A: Wh◾ch car?

B: The one I s⬭ld!

2 Practice saying this dialogue with a partner. Be sure to emphasize the focus word in each sentence.

🎧 D Pair work: Dialogues

1 Listen and practice this dialogue. Use a change in pitch and an extra long vowel sound to emphasize the underlined focus words. The stressed syllables are in **bold**.

Child at the Shoe Store

Child: I want some **shoes**.
Parent: What **kind** of shoes?
Child: The **beau**tiful kind!
Parent: **Black** or **brown**?
Child: **Nei**ther. I'm **tired** of black and brown. I want **red** shoes. **Shi**ny red shoes!

NOTE: The fourth line above has two focus words, "black" and "brown." Both focus words are emphasized.

2 Underline the focus words in the dialogue below and in the ones on the next page. Some of the sentences may have two focus words.

A Traveler

Travel Agent: Where do you want to go?
Traveler: Brazil.
Travel Agent: Where in Brazil? To the north or to the south?
Traveler: Neither. I've seen the north and south. I'm going west.

Two People on the Street

Person 1:   What are they building?

Person 2:   They're building a school.

Person 1:   What kind of school? Elementary or high school?

Person 2:   Neither. I think it's a trade school.

A Tourist

Tourist: What's the best part of Canada?

Canadian: That depends. Do you prefer the city or the countryside?

Tourist: Well, I like scenery.

Canadian: Then you should go to the Canadian Rockies.

Tourist: Do they have good shopping there?

Canadian: Maybe you'd better go to Toronto.

Two Students

Student 1: What are you doing?

Student 2: I'm studying.

Student 1: Studying what? Math or English?

Student 2: Neither. I'm sick of math and English. I'm studying nutrition, because I'm always hungry.

3 Read the dialogues out loud and practice making the focus clear.

E Music of English

1 Listen. Notice which words are the focus words.

2 Listen again and repeat each sentence until you can say it easily.

Pair work: Disagreeing and correcting

1 Listen. Notice how the focus word "month" in the second sentence is a correction for the word "week" in the first sentence.

   A: He was in Spain for a **week**.

   B: No, he was in Spain for a **month**.

2 Listen. The word "France" in the second sentence is a correction for the word "Spain" in the first sentence.

   A: He was in Spain for a **week**.

   B: No, he was in **France** for a week.

Focus Rule 6

When there is a disagreement or a correction, the word that corrects the information from the previous statement is the new focus word.

3 Practice saying these dialogues with a partner. Emphasize the underlined focus words. Take turns as Speaker A and Speaker B.

   1. A: I buy books at the **li**brary.

       B: No, you **bo**rrow books at the library.

   2. A: I buy books at the **li**brary.

       B: No, you buy books at the **book**store.

   3. A: Madrid is the capital of **Ger**many.

       B: No, it's the capital of **Spain**.

   4. A: Madrid is the capital of **Ger**many.

       B: No, Ber**lin** is the capital of Germany.

   5. A: "Actual" means "in the present **time**."

       B: No, "actual" means "**real**."

   6. A: A ship is smaller than a **boat**.

       B: I don't **think** so. A ship is **bigg**er than a boat.

   7. A: Is Dallas in Cali**for**nia?

       B: No, it's in **Tex**as.

   8. A: Is Dallas in Cali**for**nia?

       B: No, but San Fran**cis**co is in California.

G Pair work: Listening for the focus word

Student A: Say sentence **a** or sentence **b**.
Student B: Listen closely for the focus word, and say the matching response.

Example

Student A: It's a **big** dog.
Student B: No, it's really more **me**dium-sized.

OR

Student A: It's a big **dog**.
Student B: No, it's a **wolf**.

1. a. It's a big **dog**.   No, it's a **wolf**.
    b. It's a **big** dog.   No, it's really more **me**dium-sized.

2. a. But we asked for two **co**ffees!   Oh, I thought you wanted **tea**.
    b. But we asked for **two** coffees!   Oh, I thought you wanted **one**.

3. a. I thought you bought a big **car**.   No, it was a **mo**torcycle.
    b. I thought you bought a **big** car.   No, it was a **litt**le one.

4. a. Is that a silver **watch**?   No, it's a **brace**let.
    b. Is that a **sil**ver watch?   No, it's **pla**tinum.

5. a. I prefer beef **soup**.   Not **stew**?
    b. I prefer **beef** soup.   Not **chick**en?

6. a. Is there milk in the re**frig**erator?   No, it's on the **ta**ble.
    b. Is there **milk** in the refrigerator?   No, but there's **juice**.

H Pair work: Disagreement

1 Write an answer that disagrees with each of the following statements. Different answers are possible.

2 Underline the word in your answer that disagrees with the previous statement. This is the focus word of your answer.

1. A: Canada is south of the U.S.
    B: No, it's <u>north</u>.

2. A: Paris and London are countries.
    B: ....

3. A: May is the fourth month of the year.

B: ....

4. A: It's not important to study hard at school.

B: ....

5. A: India is a small country.

B: ....

3 Practice saying the dialogues with a partner.

I What was said before?

When you listen to a conversation, you may not hear what one of the speakers has just said. When this happens, listen to the emphasis in the other person's response. This can help you guess what might have been said before.

In each of the dialogues below, read Speaker B's answer. The focus word of the answer is underlined.

Can you guess what Speaker A may have said to get an answer with this emphasis? Write your guess. Different answers may be possible.

1. A: Today is Monday. ....

B: No, today is Tuesday.

2. A: ....

B: No, the wedding is on the fifth of April.

3. A: ....

B: I don't agree. We need more rain.

4. A: ....

B: But we prefer to keep the window open.

5. A: ....

B: Blue is the best color for a car.

6. A: ....

B: No, I think it's on page seven.

7. A: ....

B: No, it's the right one.

8. A: ....

B: It usually costs more than that.

J **Pair work: A disagreement**

Listen and underline the focus words. Then practice saying the dialogue with a partner.

Two Students Argue

A: I bought some books at the library.

B: They don't sell books at the library. They lend books there.
   They sell books at the bookstore. Didn't you know that?

A: On Tuesdays they sell books at the library. Surplus books.

B: Surplus?

A: Books they don't need. Extra ones.

B: I didn't know that.

A: There's a lot you don't know.

 K **Music of English**

1 Listen. Notice that the peak can go down as well as up to show emphasis.

2 Listen again and repeat each sentence until you can say it easily.

 L **Pair work: Using focus words to check information**

Here are two useful ways to ask about something you did not understand or did not hear clearly. You can emphasize a question word, or you can repeat the word you are unsure of.

1 Listen and practice being Speaker A and Speaker B.

  1. A: They got here at one o'**clock**.

      B: **When** did they get here?

  2. A: The party is on the third of **May**.

      B: The **third**?

2 Practice saying these sentences.

1. A: My **mo**ther-in-law is coming.
   B: **Who** is coming?

2. A: We're going to Hong **Kong**.
   B: **Where** are you going?

3. A: The stock market is behaving **erra**tically.
   B: The stock market is doing **what**?

4. A: All of this work will have to be finished by **Wednes**day.
   B: Finished by **when**?

5. A: We need twenty more **plates**.
   B: **Twen**ty?

6. A: We have to finish the work before **Tues**day.
   B: Be**fore** Tuesday?

7. A: I'll be **leav**ing tomorrow.
   B: To**morr**ow?

VOWEL WORK

 ## The vowel sound /ɔ/ as in "saw"

The most common pronunciations for the letter -**a**- are the relative vowel sound /æ/ as in "pan" and the alphabet vowel sound /eʸ/ as in "cake." However, there is another common vowel sound for this letter – the sound /ɔ/, as in "saw."

NOTE: In parts of Canada and the United States, /ɔ/ as in "saw" and /ɑ/ as in "top" are pronounced as the same sound. For example, some people pronounce "caught" and "cot" in the same way.

1 Listen to the sound /ɔ/ in words where the letter -**a**- is followed by -**w**-. When -**a**- is followed by the letter -**w**-, the sound of the vowel is /ɔ/ as in "saw" about 98% of the time. Repeat each word after you hear it.

saw /ɔ/

paw	dawn
jaw	prawn
law	crawl
lawn	awful
fawn	lawful

2 Listen to the sound /ɔ/ in words where the letter **-a-** is followed by **-u-**. When **-a-** is followed by the vowel letter **-u-**, it is pronounced as /ɔ/ about 89% of the time. Repeat each word after you hear it.

saw /ɔ/

cause	applaud
author	nautical
laundry	audible
caution	caught
saucer	taught

3 Listen to the sound /ɔ/ in words where the letter **-a-** is followed by the letters **-ll-** or **-lk-**. When **-a-** is followed by **-l-**, it is pronounced as /ɔ/ about 79% of the time. Repeat each word after you hear it.

saw /ɔ/

all	recall
fall	walk
ball	chalk
tall	talk
mall	stalk

4 Practice saying these sentences.

1. Who taught the baby to walk?
2. We all applauded the singers.
3. The word "nautical" means something about the sea.
4. We got up at dawn.

 Dictation

Listen and write the sentences you hear.

1. The wedding is in April.
2. ....
3. ....
4. ....
5. ....

A   **Emphasizing structure words**

As you learned in Unit 6, English speakers use contrast to emphasize the words they want their listeners to notice.

You also learned in Unit 6 that the focus word in a sentence is usually a content word and not a structure word. Structure words are de-emphasized to contrast with the words that are more important.

However, sometimes a structure word is the most important word in a sentence.

1 Listen to the following sentences. Speaker B is strongly disagreeing with Speaker A, so the structure word "am" is the most important word in Speaker B's sentence. Notice how it is emphasized.

A: You'll have to wait until you're **o**ld enough.

B: But I **a**m old enough!

2 Listen to these sentences. The structure word "and" is emphasized in Speaker B's statement because it corrects the word "or" in Speaker A's statement.

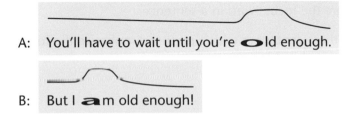

A: I think she's either sc**a**red or exc**i**ted.

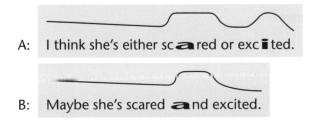

B: Maybe she's scared **a**nd excited.

> ### Focus Rule 7
>
> When a speaker feels strongly or wants to correct something that was said before, a structure word may be emphasized.

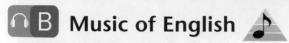

B Music of English

1 Listen. Notice in the first sentence that the structure word "and" is reduced. In the response, "and" is the focus word, so it is emphasized.

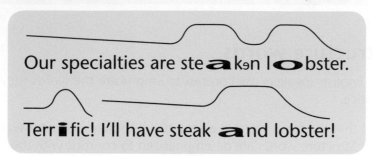

Our specialties are ste**a**k**ə**n l**o**bster.

Terr**i**fic! I'll have steak **a**nd lobster!

2 Listen again and repeat each sentence until you can say it easily.

C Pair work: Emphasizing "and" and "can"

"And" and the auxiliary verb "can" are usually reduced. However, these structure words are emphasized when they are the focus word in a sentence.

Listen. Then practice saying these sentences with a partner. Emphasize the focus words with a pitch change and a long, clear vowel sound.

1. A: Our specialties are **steak** and **lob**ster.

 B: Te**rrif**ic! I'll have steak **and** lobster!

2. A: Which is more important – in**tell**igence or **eff**ort?

 B: **Both**. You need intelligence **and** effort.

3. A: Did you call at **eight** or at **nine**?

 B: I called at eight **and** at nine.

4. A: Do you think you can do the **job**?

 B: **Yes**, I **can**!

5. A: He can write **well**.

 B: **Yes**, he **can**, when he **wants** to.

D Pair work: Emphasizing auxiliary verbs

Usually, auxiliary verbs like "do," "be," and "have" are contracted. For example, "Do you" in casual speech is usually pronounced as one syllable, "D'you." However, when an auxiliary verb is chosen as the most important word – the focus of meaning – in a sentence, it is said in its full form.

Listen to each pair of sentences on the next page, and notice how auxiliary verbs are emphasized. Then practice saying the sentences with a partner.

1. A: That's a mean **dog**.

   B: **Yes**, it **is** a mean dog, but not as mean as **mine**.

2. A: You haven't stopped by in a long **time**.

   B: **Yes**, I **have** stopped by, but you're never **here**.

3. A: I don't think the train's **leav**ing.

   B: **Sorr**y, but I see that it **is** leaving.

4. A: I'm not **go**ing.

   B: **Yes**, you **are** going!

5. A: He won't **pay** you.

   B: **Well**, I say he **will** pay me!

6. A: We're **rea**dy. Why aren't **you**?

   B: But I **am** ready.

7. A: Why don't you **like** it?

   B: But I **do** like it.

E ## Dialogue: Emphasizing "and" and auxiliary verbs

1 Read this dialogue and pay attention to the emphasis in each sentence. In some of the sentences, structure words are emphasized.

A Short Commute

(Two coworkers are talking while at the office.)

A: [1]How do you get to **work** in the morning?
   [2]Do you **walk** or ride the **bus**?

B: [3]I **walk** here. You should walk to work, **too**.
   [4]It's good **exer**cise.

A: [5]As a matter of fact, I **do** walk to work.

B: [6]But I've seen you on the **bus**!

A: [7]Maybe you **have**, but how do you suppose
   [8]I **get** to the bus? I **walk**.

B: [9]**Oh**, so you walk **and** ride the bus.

A: [10]Ex**act**ly.

2 Practice the conversation with a partner.

3 With your partner, discuss why you think structure words are emphasized in lines 5, 7, and 9. Check your answers on page 75.

Pair work: Emphasizing prepositions and pronouns

Prepositions like "in" and "on" and pronouns like "I" and "they" can be the focus word in a sentence when they correct or contrast with a word that was said before.

Listen. Notice how prepositions and pronouns are emphasized in the responses below. Then practice saying the sentences with a partner.

1. A: Is the cat on the **bed** again?

   B: **No**, she's **un**der the bed.

2. A: You forgot to leave the keys on the **desk**.

   B: I'm **sorr**y. I put them **in** the desk.

3. A: If you're going **out**, please buy some **butt**er.

   B: **Sorr**y, I'm just now coming **in**.

4. A: I'm **freez**ing.

   B: It doesn't seem cold to **me**.

5. A: Did you misplace the **keys**?

   B: **No**, **you** were the one who had them last.

6. A: Do you like to argue with your **friends**?

   B: **No**, but they like to argue with **me**.

7. A: **Hi**! What's **new**?

   B: Nothing **much**. What's new with **you**?

G Pair work: Emphasizing structure words that begin with -*h*-

You learned in Unit 7 that when a structure word, for example "his," begins with the letter -**h**-, the -**h**- is often silent. However, when this type of word is the focus word, the -**h**- is pronounced.

Practice saying the sentences with a partner. Be sure to emphasize the focus words, which are underlined.

1. A: Does she like classical **mu**sic?

   B: **No**, but **he** does.

2. A: Where's Michael's **En**glish book?

   B: **I** don't know. Ask **him**.

3. A: Jerry showed me your fine re**port**.

   B: It's not **mine**. It's mostly **his** work.

H Emphasizing pronouns

1 Listen to this poem. Some pronouns starting with the letter **-h-** are said with the full form, but some are not. Do you understand why the underlined pronouns are emphasized? Check your answer on page 75.

¹Behold the hippopotamus!
²We laugh at how he looks to us,
³And yet in moments dark and grim
⁴I wonder how <u>we</u> look to <u>him</u>.
⁵Peace, peace, thou hippopotamus!
⁶We really look all right to us,
⁷As <u>you</u> no doubt delight the eye
⁸Of other hippopotami.

– Ogden Nash

2 Practice saying the poem.

I Dialogue: Emphasizing focus words

1 Read the following dialogue. Can you explain why the speaker emphasizes structure words in lines 3, 5, and 10? The answers are on page 75.

Strange Diet

A: ¹Do you think food in this country is ex**pen**sive?

B: ²**No**, not **rea**lly.

A: ³Well, **I** think it's expensive.

B: ⁴That's because you eat in **res**taurants.

A: ⁵Where do **you** eat?

B: ⁶At **home**.

A: ⁷I didn't know you could **cook**.

B: ⁸I don't. I just eat **bread** and **tea**.

A: ⁹That isn't **sen**sible!

B: ¹⁰**Yes**, it **is** sensible. I **like** bread and tea.

A: ¹¹You're **cra**zy!

2 Practice saying the dialogue with a partner.

3 If possible, record yourself saying the dialogue with a partner. Listen to your recording. Did you emphasize the focus words?

Review: The Focus Rules

Here is a list of the focus rules you learned in Units 6 through 9.

> ## Focus Rules
>
> **1.** There is a pitch change on the vowel of the stressed syllable of the focus word. The pitch change can be up or down, but it must be a change. (Unit 6)
>
> **2.** The focus word in a short sentence or thought group is usually a content word. (Unit 6)
>
> **3.** Structure words are usually de-emphasized to help make a contrast with the focus word. (Unit 7)
>
> **4.** At the beginning of a conversation, the focus word is usually the last content word in a thought group (a short sentence, clause, or phrase). (Unit 8)
>
> **5.** After a conversation begins, any word can become a new thought (the new focus of information). (Unit 8)
>
> **6.** When there is a disagreement or a correction, the word that corrects the information from the previous statement is the new focus word. (Unit 8)
>
> **7.** When a speaker feels strongly or wants to correct something that was said before, a structure word may be emphasized. (Unit 9)

VOWEL WORK

 Different vowel sounds for the letter -*a*-

You have learned three vowel sounds for the letter -**a**-. These sounds are /eʸ/ as in "cake," /æ/ as in "pan," and /ɔ/ as in "saw."

Listen and circle the word you hear.

cake /eʸ/	pan /æ/	saw /ɔ/
1. paid	pad	pawed
2. pain	pan	pawn
3. pained	panned	pawned
4. take	tack	talk
5. bake	back	balk
6. stake	stack	stalk
7. Kate	cat	caught

(In row 1, "pawed" is circled.)

L

The contrast between /ɔ/ and /ɑ/

Listen and circle the word you hear.

NOTE: In some parts of Canada and the United States, /ɔ/ and /ɑ/ are pronounced as the same sound, so words like "caught" and "cot" sound the same. However, if you are listening to somebody using this contrast, you will understand the speaker better if you have practiced saying the contrast.

saw /ɔ/	top /ɑ/
1. stalk	(stock)
2. dawn	Don
3. caught	cot
4. pawed	pod
5. pawned	pond

 M

Dictation

Listen and write the sentences you hear.

1. I'm afraid I cannot agree. ....

2. ....

3. ....

4. ....

5. ....

Answers to Tasks E, H, and I

Task E (page 71)

3 In line 5, "do" is emphasized because it contrasts with "should" in line 3.

In line 7, "have" is emphasized because the speaker is disagreeing strongly with the statement in line 6.

In line 9, "and" is emphasized because the speaker now realizes that they are both right. Here "and" contrasts with "or" in line 2.

Task H (page 73)

1 The underlined pronouns are emphasized because they contrast with other pronouns.

"We" and "him" in line 4 contrast with "he" and "us" in line 2.

"You" in line 7 contrasts with "we" in line 6.

Task I (page 73)

1 The pronouns in lines 3 and 5 are in contrast to the pronouns in lines 1 and 4.

In line 10, "is" contrasts with "isn't" in line 9.

A | ## Introducing continuants and stops

You have been practicing vowel sounds in Units 2 through 9. However, consonant sounds are also important, especially for grammar cues at the end of words, such as the sound **/s/** in "books" to show plural.

1 Look at the parts of the mouth in this picture.

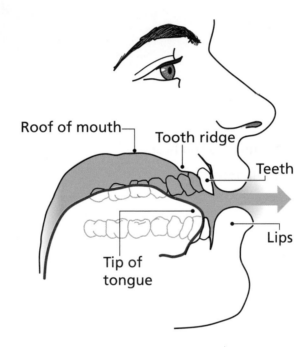

Different speech sounds are made by the way air flows out over the tongue. When the tongue touches different parts of the mouth, consonants are formed. The change in airflow changes the sound.

2 For many sounds we let the air flow through the mouth without stopping. These sounds are called **_continuants._**

Listen to this word and notice how the final sound continues.

bussss

3 In other sounds, we stop the airflow inside the mouth. These sounds are called **_stops_**.

Listen to this word and notice how the final sound stops.

but

4 Look at pictures of the continuing sound **/s/** and the stop sound **/t/**, seen from different directions.

bus_ /s/   but_ /t/

Looking from the side

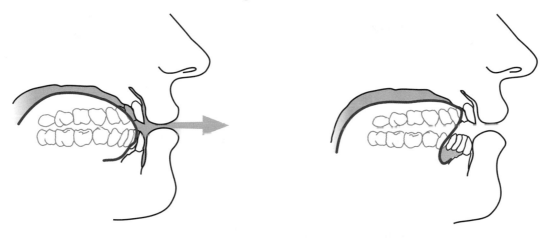

Looking to the front

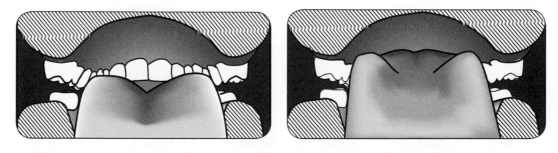

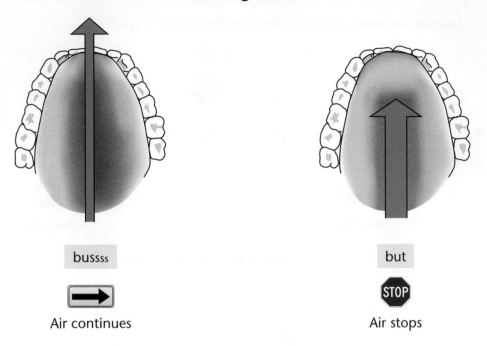

bussss	but
➡️	🛑 STOP
Air continues	Air stops

B Saying /s/ and /t/

1 Whisper the words "bus" and "but," and feel the difference between the final **/s/** sound and the final **/t/** sound. During **/s/**, you can feel the air flow out. For **/t/**, the air is stopped.

2 Practice saying these words.

bus but bus but

🎧 C Which word is different?

Listen. Mark the column for the word that is different.

	X	Y	Z	
1.	....	....	.......✔........	(lice, lice, light)
2.	....	....	....	
3.	....	....	....	
4.	....	....	....	
5.	....	....	....	
6.	....	....	....	
7.	....	....	....	
8.	....	....	....	

D Which word do you hear?

1 Listen. Circle the word you hear.

NOTE: Sometimes the letter **-c-** is pronounced **/s/** as in "race" and "rice."

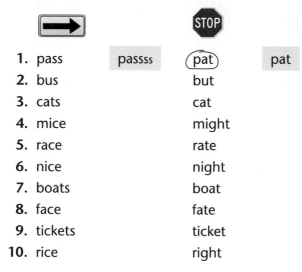

1. pass	passsss	(pat)	pat
2. bus		but	
3. cats		cat	
4. mice		might	
5. race		rate	
6. nice		night	
7. boats		boat	
8. face		fate	
9. tickets		ticket	
10. rice		right	

2 Practice saying the words you circled.

E Music of English

1 Listen. Notice that a final **/s/** sound can mean the **_plural_** of a word.

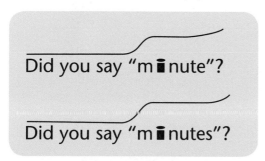

Did you say "m i nute"?

Did you say "m i nutes"?

2 Listen again and repeat each question until you can say it easily.

F Pair work: Singular and plural words

The continuant sound **/s/** is often used at the end of a word to make it plural.

Student A: Say a word from each pair of words on the next page.

Student B: If the word is singular hold up one finger. If the word is plural, hold up all five fingers.

Take turns choosing a word to say.

Examples

Student A: Minutes

Student B: (Hold up five fingers.)

Student A: Night.

Student B: (Hold up one finger.)

1. minutes	minute
2. nights	night
3. lights	light
4. tickets	ticket
5. jackets	jacket
6. seats	seat
7. mats	mat
8. boats	boat

G Pair work: Is it singular or plural?

Student A: Say sentence **a** or sentence **b**.

Student B: Say "singular" or "plural."

Take turns saying the sentences.

Examples

Student A: Read your books.

Student B: Plural.

1. a. Read your book.

 b. Read your books.

2. a. Bring your map tomorrow.

 b. Bring your maps tomorrow.

3. a. Copy your report every day.

 b. Copy your reports every day.

4. a. I put the ticket in my pocket.

 b. I put the tickets in my pocket.

5. a. Where did you put the cake?

 b. Where did you put the cakes?

6. a. Did you enjoy your trip?

b. Did you enjoy your trips?

7. a. Please clean the mat now.

b. Please clean the mats now.

8. a. Fill the bucket with hot water.

b. Fill the buckets with hot water.

H Pair work: Saying sentences with /s/ and /t/

Student A: Ask question **a** or question **b**.

Student B: Say the matching answer.

Take turns asking the questions.

Example

Student A: How do you spell "night"?

Student B: N - I - G - H - T.

1. a. How do you spell "night"?   N - I - G - H - T.

b. How do you spell "nice"?   N - I - C - E.

2. a. How do you spell "bought"?   B - O - U - G - H - T.

b. How do you spell "boss"?   B - O - S - S.

3. a. What does "mice" mean?   The plural of "mouse."

b. What does "might" mean?   "Power."

4. a. Do you have the tickets?   Yes, they're in my pocket.

b. Do you have the ticket?   Yes, it's in my pocket.

5. a. How do you spell "right"?   R - I - G - H - T.

b. How do you spell "rice"?   R - I - C - E.

6. a. What does "less" mean?   The opposite of "more."

b. What does "let" mean?   To allow.

7. a. Did you buy the coats?   Yes, one for each of us.

b. Did you buy the coat?   Yes, I'm wearing it.

8. a. Did you say "minute"?   No, I said "second."

b. Did you say "minutes"?   Yes, ten minutes.

🎧 I Linking with /s/ 🔗

When a word ends in the continuant sound **/s/**, the final **/s/** links to a vowel at the beginning of the next word. There is no pause between the two words.

less of   lessssof

1 Listen and repeat these words. Link the final **/s/** to the vowel at the beginning of the next word.

less of	lessssof
pass it	passssit
Miss Anderson	MissssAnderson

2 Practice linking with these sentences.

1. The boats entered the water.   boatsssentered
2. The coats all need to be cleaned.   coatsssall
3. The tickets are in my pocket.   ticketsssare
4. Is the boss in the office?   bossssin
5. The nights are long here.   nightsssare

🎧 J Linking with /t/ 🔗

When a word ends in the stop sound **/t/**, the final **/t/** links to a vowel at the beginning of the next word.

get in   getin

1 Listen and repeat these linked words. Notice that when **/t/** links with a vowel, it is said quickly and sounds like **/d/**.

get in	getin
right answer	rightanswer
great ending	greatending

2 Practice linking with these sentences.

1. The boat entered the water.   boatentered
2. We need a lot of money.   needalotof
3. It's right around the corner.   rightaround
4. We bought everything we could carry.   boughteverything
5. The bucket is empty.   bucketis

VOWEL WORK

 K ## Practicing vowels with /s/ and /t/

1 Listen and circle the word you hear.

Words ending in /t/

1.	ate	(at)	ought
2.	bait	bat	bought
3.	Kate	cat	caught
4.	rate	rat	right
5.	mate	meet	might

Words ending in /s/

6.	base	bass	boss
7.	mace	mass	mice
8.	lace	lease	lice
9.	moose	mouse	moss
10.	pace	pass	peace

2 Practice saying the words you circled.

 L ## Dictation

Listen and write the sentences you hear.

1. The tickets are in his pocket.

2.

3.

4.

5.

A Continuants and stops: /r/ and /d/

The **/r/** sound is a continuant. When making this sound, the air flows out along the middle of the tongue without stopping.

1 Listen to this word and pay attention to the final **/r/** sound.

nearrrr

2 Listen to this word and pay attention to the final sound. It is the stop sound **/d/**.

need

STOP

3 The pictures on the left sides of this page and the next page show the continuant sound **/r/**. Compare these with the pictures on the right sides of this page and the next page for the stop sound **/d/**.

near_ /r/   nee**d** /d/

Looking from the side

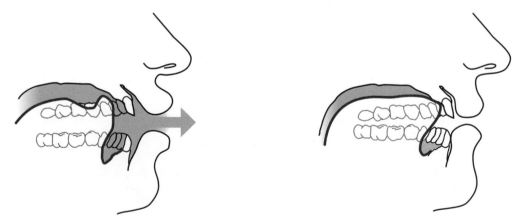

Looking to the front

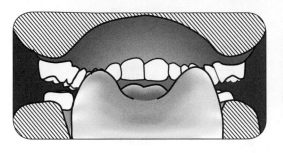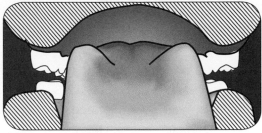

Looking down

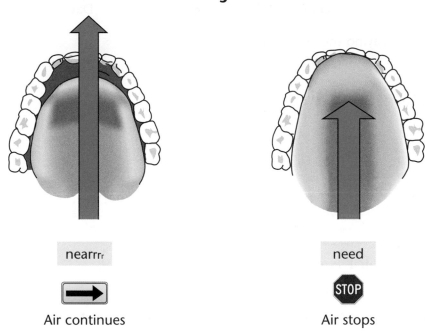

nearrrᵣ

Air continues

need

STOP

Air stops

B Saying /r/ and /d/

1 Silently do this:

- Raise your tongue so that you feel the sides of the tongue touch the upper tooth ridge toward the back of your mouth.
- Do not let the tip of your tongue touch the roof of your mouth.

This is the position for the continuant sound **/r/**.

2 Silently raise your whole tongue so that you are pressing the tooth ridge all around and the air cannot flow out. This is the position for the stop sound **/d/**.

3 Experiment by whispering "hire, hide, hire, hide" several times. Make a clear contrast between the continuant and the stop. Then say the words out loud.

C Which word do you hear?

1 Listen. Circle the word you hear.

Final sound			Beginning sound	
→	STOP		→	STOP
1. (near)	need		5. real	deal
2. fear	feed		6. roam	dome
3. pair	paid		7. rent	dent
4. core	code		8. rave	Dave

2 Practice saying the words you circled.

D Music of English ♪

1 Listen.

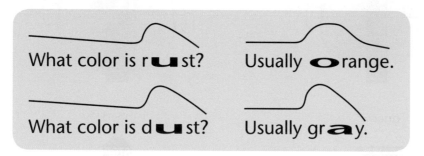

What color is r**u**st?   Usually **o**range.

What color is d**u**st?   Usually gr**a**y.

2 Listen again and repeat each sentence until you can say it easily.

E Pair work: Saying sentences with /r/ and /d/

Student A: Ask question **a** or question **b**.

Student B: Say the answer that matches the question.

Example

Student A: What color is dust?

Student B: Usually gray.

1. a. What color is rust?   Usually orange.
   b. What color is dust?   Usually gray.

2. a. How do you spell "rare"?   R - A - R - F
   b. How do you spell "dare"?   D - A - R - E.

3. a. What's a dam?   A wall for water.
   b. What's a ram?   A male sheep.

4. a. What does "fear" mean? Feeling scared.
   b. What does "feed" mean? To give food.

5. a. What's the definition of "liar"?   A person who tells lies.
   b. What's the definition of "dire"?   Extremely serious.

6. a. What does "we're" mean?   "We are."
   b. What does "weed" mean?   A plant nobody wants.

7. a. What's the definition of "lie"?   The opposite of "truth."
   b. What's the definition of "die"?   To stop living.

8. a. How do you spell "explode"?   E - X - P - L - O - D - E.
   b. How do you spell "explore"?   E - X - P - L - O - R - E.

F Linking with /r/

When a word ends in the continuant sound /r/, the final /r/ links to a vowel sound at the beginning of the next word.

hear us   hearrrus

NOTE: Many English words end in a silent letter -e-. Linking sounds go right over the silent -e-. For example, "where are" sounds like   wherrrare .

1 Listen and repeat these linked words.

hear us   hearrrus

pair of shoes   pairrrof shoes

her arm   herrrarm

2 Read the following sentences and draw linking marks connecting words that end in the /r/ sound to words that begin with a vowel sound.

   1. Did you hear us?
   2. There isn't a better answer.
   3. I plan to retire early.
   4. They share everything.
   5. We're all here in the car.
   6. Her answer is more interesting.

3 Practice saying the sentences. Be sure to link with the /r/ sound.

⌒G Linking with /d/ ⌒⌒⌒

When a word ends in the stop sound **/d/**, the final **/d/** links to a vowel at the beginning of the next word. This makes it sound as if the final **/d/** is the beginning of the next word. For example, "paid Ann" sounds close to "pay Dan."

paid‿Ann	paidAnn
had‿it	hadit

1 Listen and repeat these linked words.

paid‿Ann	paidAnn
I had‿it	I hadit
answered‿everyone	answeredeveryone

2 Read the following sentences and draw linking marks connecting words that end in the **/d/** sound to words that begin with a vowel sound.

1. I told‿everybody.
2. She said everything.
3. They made us do all the work.
4. The parade always starts early.
5. I did only the first part.
6. She had always wanted us to sing.
7. We tried our best.
8. Her grade is perfect.

3 Practice saying the sentences. Be sure to link with the **/d/** sound.

⌒H The sound combination /rd/

1 Listen and circle the word you hear. This combination of consonants at the end of verbs usually means *past tense*.

1. (cheer)   cheered
2. her   heard
3. share   shared
4. prepare   prepared
5. hire   hired
6. retire   retired
7. bore   bored
8. care   cared

2 Practice saying the words you circled.

Pair work: Past or present?

A final /d/ sound is often used to make a verb past tense.

Student A: Say sentence **a** or sentence **b**.
Student B: Say "past" or "present."

Example

Student A: We shared all the food.
Student B: Past.

1. a. We share all the food.
    b. We shared all the food.

2. a. The dogs scare every cat.
    b. The dogs scared every cat.

3. a. Some speakers bore us.
    b. Some speakers bored us.

4. a. They hire new employees on Friday.
    b. They hired new employees on Friday.

5. a. They fear every animal.
    b. They feared every animal.

6. a. The children share all the cookies.
    b. The children shared all the cookies.

7. a. We admire all your work.
    b. We admired all your work.

8. a. They pour milk into the glass.
    b. They poured milk into the glass.

 # Continuants and stops: /l/ and /d/

1 The sound /l/ is another continuant sound. Listen to the word "bell," and pay close attention to the /l/ sound at the end of the word.

belllll

2 Compare these pictures of the continuant sound /l/ and the stop sound /d/.

bell /l/

bed /d/

Looking from the side

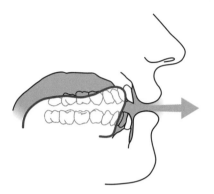
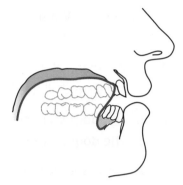

Looking to the front

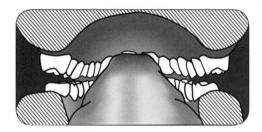

Looking down

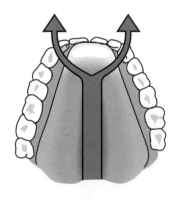
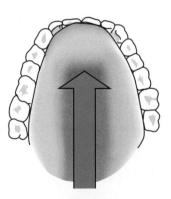

bellllı

bed

Air continues

Air stops

3 Silently make an **/l/** sound this way: Keep the tip of your tongue pressed against the tooth ridge at the front of your mouth, but lower the rest of the tongue. This allows the air to flow over the tongue and out on both sides of the raised tip. If you breathe in strongly, instead of out, you will feel the cold air coming back in over the sides of the tongue.

4 Practice the position for the **/d/** sound again.

5 Experiment by whispering "bell, bed, bell, bed" several times. Then say the words out loud.

K Which word do you hear?

Listen. Circle the word you hear.

Final sound		Beginning sound	
→	STOP	→	STOP
1. bell	(bed)	6. lid	did
2. sell	said	7. late	date
3. spell	spelled	8. lime	dime
4. tail	failed	9. loom	doom
5. mail	maid	10. lawn	dawn

L Pair work: Saying words with final /l/ and /d/

Student A: Say a word from each pair of words.
Student B: Say the other word in the pair.

Example

Student A: Wide.
Student B: While.

→	STOP		→	STOP
1. while	wide		5. roll	road
2. rail	raid		6. mail	made
3. real	read		7. feel	feed
4. they'll	they'd		8. I'll	I'd

Pair work: Saying sentences with final /l/ and /d/

Student A: Say question **a** or question **b**.
Student B: Say the matching answer.

Example

Student A: How do you spell "kneel"?
Student B: K - N - E - E - L.

1. a. How do you spell "need"?   N - E - E - D.
   b. How do you spell "kneel"?   K - N - E - E - L.

2. a. What does "they'll" mean?   "They will."
   b. What does "they'd" mean?   "They would" or "they had."

3. a. What does "rule" mean?   To govern.
   b. What does "rude" mean?   Not polite.

4. a. What does "fell" mean?   The past of "fall."
   b. What does "fed" mean?   The past of "feed."

5. a. What's the opposite of "well"?   "Sick."
   b. What's the opposite of "wed"?   "Unmarried."

6. a. How do you spell "seal"?   S - E - A - L.
   b. How do you spell "seed"?   S - E - E - D.

7. a. Why did she feed it?   It was hungry.
   b. Why did she feel it?   To see if it was hot.

8. a. What does "I'll" mean?   "I will."
   b. What does "I'd" mean?   "I had."

 Linking with /l/ ⌬⌬⌬

Words that end with the continuant sound /l/ link with words that begin with a vowel.
For example, when the words "all eyes" are said together, it sounds like "all lies."

1 Listen and repeat these linked words.

sell everything   sellIIeverything

feel excited   feelIIexcited

I'll always   I'llIIalways

2 Read the following sentences and draw linking marks connecting words that end in the /l/ sound to words that begin with a vowel sound.

1. We want to sell everything.
2. Please tell us the news.
3. Are you well enough to work?
4. We have to pull up all the flowers before it snows.
5. I'll always call Allen on his birthday.

3 Practice saying the sentences. Be sure to link with the /l/ sound.

Contractions with final /l/ and /d/

The auxiliary verbs "will," "would," and "did" are usually contracted in spoken English. For this reason, it is important for you to be able to hear the /l/ or /d/ sound at the end of words.

I would eat. ⟶ I'd eat.
I will eat. ⟶ I'll eat.

Listen. You will hear either sentence **a** or sentence **b**. Circle the full form of the contraction you hear.

	Contraction	**Full Form**
1. a.	They'll ask a good question.	(They will)
b.	They'd ask a good question.	They would
2. a.	He'll answer soon.	He will
b.	He'd answer soon.	He would
3. a.	Do you think they'll like it?	They will
b.	Do you think they'd like it?	They would
4. a.	I said I'll do the work.	I will
b.	I said I'd do the work.	I would
5. a.	Who'll they ask?	Who will
b.	Who'd they ask?	Who did
6. a.	Where'll Ann find one?	Where will
b.	Where'd Ann find one?	Where did

The sound combination /ld/

Listen and repeat the words below. Concentrate on the combination of sounds at the end of each word.

filled	told
sold	spelled
failed	smiled
called	sailed

 Music of English 🎵▲

1 Listen.

NOTE: The first **-c-** in "succeed" is pronounced with the stop sound **/k/**. The second **-c-** in "succeed" is pronounced with the continuant sound **/s/**.

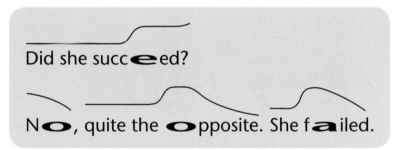

2 Listen again and repeat each sentence until you can say it easily. Be sure to emphasize the focus words and end them with a stop sound.

R **Pair work: Past or present?**

Student A: Say sentence **a** or sentence **b**.
Student B: Say "past" or "present."

Pay close attention to the final sound of the verb.

Example

Student A: We failed every time.
Student B: Past.

1. a. We fail every time.
   b. We failed every time.

2. a. They close everything.
   b. They closed everything.

3. a. I call you every night.
   b. I called you every night.

4. a. They usually stay late.
   b. They usually stayed late.

5. a. They arrive at six o'clock.
   b. They arrived at six o'clock.

6. a. We save all your stuff.
   b. We saved all your stuff.

7. a. They bore us.
   b. They bored us.

8. a. The children spill their juice.
   b. The children spilled their juice.

VOWEL WORK

S Using the Vowel Rules with /r/, /d/, and /l/

Use the One Vowel Rule (see page 14) and the Two Vowel Rule (see page 12) to decide how these words are pronounced. Practice saying each word.

Beginning /r/, /d/, and /l/

rake	rack	dine	din	lied	lid
ripe	rip	dame	dam	lease	less
reed	red	dime	dim	like	lick
ride	rid	duel	dull	laid	lad

Final /d/ and /l/

fade	fad	pile	pill
died	did	seal	sell
code	cod	mule	mull
bleed	bled	feel	fell
node	nod	pale	pal

Practicing vowels with /r/, /d/, and /l/

1 Listen and circle the words you hear.

NOTE: Vowel sounds change a little when followed by an **/r/** sound.

Words ending in /r/

1. fear fair (fire)
2. pure pair peer
3. hear hair hire
4. cure core care

Words ending in /d/

5. seed side sad
6. feed fade fad
7. rude rode rod
8. reed raid ride

Words ending in /l/

9. feel fail file
10. pal pale pill
11. meal mill mile
12. rail role rule

2 Practice saying the words you circled.

A **Introducing voicing**

1 Listen to the words "hiss" and "buzz."

This is the sound a snake makes:

hiss   hissss

This is the sound a bee makes:

buzz

2 Press your fingers against the opening of your ears, and say the word "hiss," continuing the final **/s/** sound until you hear it clearly.

3 Press your fingers against the opening of your ears and say the word "buzz," continuing the final **/z/** sound until you hear the difference from the **/s/** sound.

The buzzing of the **/z/** sound is called **voicing**. **/z/** is a voiced sound. **/s/** is a voiceless sound.

NOTE: When you whisper, you are not voicing any sounds.

4 Practice saying each sound, switching back and forth until you can hear the difference between the voiced and voiceless sounds.

/s/	/z/	/s/	/z/
Ssss	Zzzz	Ssss	Zzzz

∩B Saying words with /s/ and /z/

Listen and repeat each pair of words.

NOTE: The letter **-s-** is sometimes pronounced **/z/** as in "eyes" and "his."

Voiceless sound /s/		Voiced sound /z/	
Beginning sound			
sip	sip	zip	zip
sink		zinc	
Sue		zoo	
seal		zeal	
Final sound			
bus	bus	buzz	buzz
fuss		fuzz	
place		plays	
miss		Ms.	
Middle sound			
fussy	fussy	fuzzy	fuzzy
busing		buzzing	
racing		raising	
facing		phasing	

∩C Which word is different?

Listen. Mark the column for the word that is different.

	X	Y	Z	
1.	....	....	......✔.........	(eyes, eyes, ice)
2.	....	....	....	
3.	....	....	....	
4.	....	....	....	
5.	....	....	....	
6.	....	....	....	
7.	....	....	....	
8.	....	....	....	

D Linking with /s/ and /z/ 🔗

Practice saying these sentences. Link words that end in the **/s/** and **/z/** sounds to words that begin with a vowel sound.

Linking with /s/

1. Snakes hiss out of fear.   Snakes hissssout of fear.

2. Billy left a mess in the sink.   Billy left a messssin the sink.

3. How nice of you to come!

4. Would you like a piece of pie?

Linking with /z/

5. His aunt called.   Hizzzaunt called.

6. Has everybody left?   Hazzzeverybody left?

7. My eyes are tired.

8. Where's Anne?

🎧 E Saying phrases with /s/ and /z/

Listen and repeat each word or phrase.

Voiceless sound /s/

1. hissing sound
2. snake
3. a sand snake
4. That's harmless.

Voiced sound /z/

5. buzzing noise
6. bees in the desert
7. amazing
8. Amazing, isn't it?

Voiceless sound /s/ and voiced sound /z/

9. sounds like bees   soundz like beez

10. hissing noise   hissing noize

11. That's amazing.   That's amazing .

12. A poisonous snake?   A poizonous snake ?

1 Listen. Notice that the letter **-s-** in "that's" is voiceless and the letter **-s-** in "isn't" is voiced. Also notice that this sentence has two focus words.

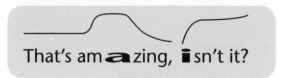

That's am**a**zing, **i**sn't it?

2 Listen again and repeat the sentence until you can say it easily. Be sure to make a contrast between the voiced and voiceless sounds.

G Pair work: Dialogue

Practice this conversation with a partner.

In the Desert

A: What's that buzzing noise?

B: It sounds like bees.

A: That's amazing, isn't it?

B: Not really. There are flowers and bees in the desert.

A: What's that hissing sound?

B: Sounds like a snake.

A: A snake! A poisonous snake?

B: No, it's a sand snake. They're harmless.

H The sounds /f/ and /v/

1 Listen to the sound **/f/** in "leaf" and the sound **/v/** in "leave."

| leaf | leaf |
| leave | leave |

2 Look at this picture of the mouth position for the sounds **/f/** and **/v/**. In both sounds, the upper teeth touch the back of the lower lip. The position is the same for the two sounds, but **/f/** is voiceless and **/v/** is voiced.

Looking from the side

/f/ and /v/

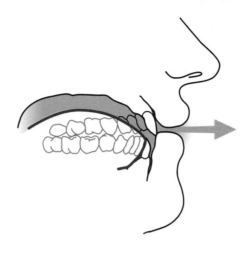

 ## Saying words with /f/ and /v/

Listen and repeat the following pairs of words.

Voiceless sound /f/		Voiced sound /v/	
Final sound			
leaf	leaf	leave	leave
half	half	have	have
safe	safe	save	save
Beginning sound			
fat	fat	vat	vat
fine	fine	vine	vine
fault	fault	vault	vault

J Pair work: Saying words with /f/ and /v/

Student A: Say a word from each pair of words.
Student B: Say "voiced" or "voiceless."
Student A: If the answer is wrong, repeat the word so your partner can try again.

Take turns saying the words.

Example

Student A: Van.
Student B: Voiceless.
Student A: No. Van.
Student B: Oh, it's voiced.

Beginning sound

Voiceless	Voiced
1. fan	van
2. fine	vine
3. fail	veil
4. fast	vast
5. ferry	very

Final sound

Voiceless	Voiced
6. leaf	leave
7. safe	save
8. half	have
9. proof	prove
10. belief	believe

Middle sound

Voiceless	Voiced
11. leafing	leaving
12. surface	service
13. rifle	rival
14. reference	reverence

K Pair work: Asking questions with /f/ and /v/

Student A: Ask question **a** or question **b**.
Student B: Say the matching answer.
Student A: If the answer is wrong, repeat the question.

Take turns asking the questions.

Examples

Student A: What does "vine" mean?
Student B: A kind of plant.

Student A: What does "veil" mean?
Student B: The opposite of "succeed."
Student A: No. What does "veil" mean?
Student B: A covering for the face.

1. a. What does "fine" mean?   Something like "good."
   b. What does "vine" mean?   A kind of plant.

2. a. What does "veil" mean?   A covering for the face.
   b. What does "fail" mean?   The opposite of "succeed."

3. a. How do you spell "have"?   H - A - V - E.
   b. How do you spell "half"?   H - A - L - F.

4. a. What's a "v"?   A letter of the alphabet.
   b. What's a "fee"?   The cost for a service.

5. a. How do you spell "believe"?   B - E - L - I - E - V - E.
   b. How do you spell "belief"?   B - E - L - I - E - F.

6. a. What does "fear" mean?   To be afraid.
   b. What does "veer" mean?   To change direction fast.

7. a. Do you have a view?   Yes, I can see the lake.
   b. Do you have a few?   No, I don't have any.

8. a. What's a "volley"?   A shot in tennis.
   b. What's a "folly"?   A foolish act.

Voiced and voiceless sounds for the spelling -*th*-

Listen. Notice the contrast between the letter combination -**th**- when it is voiced and when it is voiceless.

teeth	teeth	teethe	tee**the**
bath	bath	bathe	ba**the**

The symbol for the voiceless -**th**- sound is /θ/, and the symbol for the voiced -**th**- sound is /ð/.

 ## Voiceless -*th*-

Listen and repeat these words. In all of these words, the letters -**th**- are pronounced with the voiceless sound /θ/.

Final sound	Beginning sound
teeth	thing
path	thought
math	thief
tooth	thunder

 ## Voiced -*th*-

1 Listen to the words below. Circle the words that have a voiced /ð/ sound for the letters -**th**-.

1. (bathe)
2. breath
3. breathe
4. math
5. they
6. think
7. thigh
8. this

2 Practice saying the words above.

O Linking with /f/, /v/, and the -th- sounds ⚭⚭⚭

Practice saying these sentences. Link words that end in the /f/, /v/, and /θ/ or /ð/ sounds to words that begin with a vowel sound.

NOTE: The spelling -**gh**- is often pronounced /f/ as in "laugh."

Voiceless final sounds

1. They laugh a lot.
2. Both are ready.
3. It's half empty.
4. Take a bath in hot water.
5. Read the fourth unit.
6. We know enough about it.

Voiced final sounds

7. Have a seat.
8. Save all your money.
9. Prove it.
10. Don't give up.
11. Breathe in slowly.
12. Bathe in cold water.

P Linking continuants ⚭⚭⚭

You have already practiced linking final voiced and voiceless continuant sounds like /z/, /s/, /v/, /f/, /ð/, and /θ/ to vowel sounds at the beginning of the next word. Final continuant sounds can also link with beginning continuant sounds.

1 Listen and repeat these words. Do not pause between the linked sounds.

his land	hi**zzz**land
bus stop	bus**sss**stop
have money	ha**vvv**money

2 Practice saying these sentences. Link words that end in a continuant sound to words that begin with a continuant sound.

1. His money's not here.   His**zzz**money**zzz**not here.
2. She wants seven.   She wants**sss**seven .
3. Let me know if Sam calls.   Let me know if**ff**Sam calls.
4. Excuse me.
5. I save letters.
6. We went with Sue.
7. Does she always laugh so loudly?

Review: Voiced and voiceless sounds for *-th-*

1 Listen to this limerick. Circle the words that begin with **-th-**.

> The teachers are quick to suggest
> That we study quite hard for a test.
> It takes lots of thought
> To learn what we're taught,
> So I think I'd prefer just to rest.

2 Read the limerick aloud several times. The sound of **-th-** in "the" and "that" should be the voiced sound /ð/. The sound of **-th-** in "thought" and "think" should be the voiceless sound /θ/.

R Pair work: Nouns and verbs

Student A: Say a noun or verb from each pair of words below.
Student B: Say "noun" or "verb."

Examples

Student A: Prove.
Student B: Verb.

Student A: Teeth.
Student B: Noun.

NOTE: The verbs below end with a voiced sound, and the nouns end with a voiceless sound.

Verbs		Nouns		Verbs		Nouns	
prove	pro**v**e	proof	proof	advise	advi**z**e	advice	advice
save		safe		excuse		excuse	
teethe		teeth		believe		belief	
use		use		relieve		relief	

/aʸ/

vi**zz**z

advise

Can you advise me?

/aʸ/

vis

advice

That's good advice.

Pair work: Review of contractions with /v/, /d/, and /l/

Student A: Say sentence **a**, **b**, or **c**.
Student B: Say the full form of the contraction.

Take turns saying the sentences.

Example

Student A: They'd gone.
Student B: They had.

Contraction	**Full form**
1. a. They've gone.	they have
b. They'd gone.	they had
2. a. We'd eaten.	we had
b. We've eaten.	we have
3. a. Where'd you put it?	where did
b. Where'll you put it?	where will
c. Where've you put it?	where have
4. a. We'll come.	we will
b. We'd come.	we had
c. We've come.	we have
5. a. How've you come here?	how have
b. How'd you come here?	how did
c. How'll you come here?	how will
6. a. We'll shut the door.	we will
b. We'd shut the door.	we had
c. We've shut the door.	we have
7. a. They've put it away.	they have
b. They'll put it away.	they will
c. They'd put it away.	they had
8. a. Why'll you come?	why will
b. Why'd you come?	why did
c. Why've you come?	why have

VOWEL WORK

 T ## The vowel sound /ɔʸ/ as in "boy" and "coin"

In stressed syllables, the spelling **-oy-** is pronounced with the sound /ɔʸ/ as in "boy" 100% of the time, and the spelling **-oi-** is pronounced with the sound /ɔʸ/ as in "coin" about 85% of the time.

1 Listen and repeat these words with **-oy-** pronounced /ɔʸ/.

boy /ɔʸ/

joy	enjoy
boy	royal
toys	voyage
annoys	enjoyment

2 Listen and repeat these words with **-oi-** pronounced /ɔʸ/.

coin /ɔʸ/

join	poison
noise	ointment
voice	avoid
choice	disappoint

3 Practice saying these sentences.

1. The king is enjoying his royal voyage.
2. She found employment selling noisy toys.
3. You can avoid disappointment by joining our team.

 U ## Dictation

Listen and write the sentences you hear.

1. Fall leaves are bright red.

2. ....

3. ....

4. ....

5. ....

13 | Voicing and Syllable Length
Aspiration

 A ## Introducing voicing and syllable length

The final sound of an English word is important because it may be a grammar signal. For example, the final consonant in a word may tell you if the word is a noun or a verb.

Final consonants are sometimes hard to hear, but there is an extra signal to help the listener know if the final consonant in a word is voiced or voiceless.

1 Listen to the words "save" and "safe." "Save" ends in a voiced consonant, and "safe" ends in a voiceless consonant. There is also another difference between these words. Can you hear it?

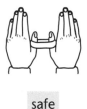

s**a**ve

safe

2 Listen to the words again. Pay attention to the vowel sound in each word. The vowel sound in "save" is longer than the vowel sound in "safe." This contrast in length of the vowel helps the listener recognize which word was said.

Rule for Vowels Followed by a Voiced Consonant

A vowel before a voiced consonant is longer than a vowel before a voiceless consonant.

B Pair work: Final voiced and voiceless continuants

Student A: Say a word from each pair below.
Student B: Say the other word in the pair.

Be sure to make the vowel extra long in a word that ends in a voiced continuant.

Example

Student A: Save.
Student B: Safe.

          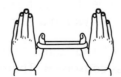

Voiceless continuant   **Voiced continuant**

safe	safe	save	s**a**ve
cease	cease	seize	s**e**ize
fuss	fuss	fuzz	f**u**zz
leaf	leaf	leave	l**e**ave
bus		buzz	
race		rays	
half		have	
Miss		Ms.	
price		prize	

C Which word is different?

Listen. Mark the column for the word that is different.

1. ....✔........ (save, save, safe)
2. ....
3. ....
4. ....
5. ....
6. ....
7. ....
8. ....

D Final voiced and voiceless stops

It is often difficult to hear final stop sounds in the speech of North Americans from the United States and Canada. For this reason, it is particularly important to notice the length of the vowel sound before the final stop. A lengthened vowel means that the final stop is voiced.

Practice saying these pairs of words. Be sure to lengthen the vowel before a final voiced stop.

Voiceless stop /t/

bet   bet
sat
debt
right

Voiced stop /d/

bed   b**e**d
sad
dead
ride

Voiceless stop /k/

back   back
rack
duck
pick

Voiced stop /g/

bag   b**a**g
rag
dug
pig

Voiceless stop /p/

cap   cap
rope
lap
mop

Voiced stop /b/

cab   c**a**b
robe
lab
mob

E Pair work: Final voiced and voiceless consonants in sentences

Student A: Say sentence **a** or sentence **b**. Add length to the vowel if you choose the sentence with a voiced final consonant.

Student B: Say the matching answer.

NOTE: The sentences continue on the next page.

Example

Student A: He wants peas.
Student B: Not carrots?

1. a. He wants peas.   Not carrots?
   b. He wants peace.   Not war?

2. a. There's something in my eyes!   Call a doctor!
   b. There's something in my ice!   Call a waiter.

3. a. Is it in the bag?

No, in the box.

   b. Is it in the back?

No, in the front.

4. a. Isn't this a good prize?

Yes, did you win it?

   b. Isn't this a good price?

Yes, it's really cheap.

5. a. What kind of word is "prove"?

It's a verb.

   b. What kind of word is "proof"?

It's a noun.

6. a. What's a buck?

A dollar.

   b. What's a bug?

An insect.

7. a. What does "Miss" mean?

An unmarried woman.

   b. What does "Ms." mean?

A woman.

8. a. What does "wrote" mean?

The past tense of "write."

   b. What does "rode" mean?

The past tense of "ride."

9. a. What's a rope for?

To tie something up.

   b. What's a robe for?

To keep you warm.

 ## F Noun or verb?

In the lists below, the verbs end with voiced consonants and the nouns end with voiceless consonants. Therefore, the verbs have a longer vowel sound before the final consonant.

1 Listen. Circle the noun or verb you hear.

Verbs	Nouns		Verbs	Nouns
1. (prove) /v/	proof /f/	6. believe /v/	belief /f/
2. save /v/	safe /f/	7. devise /z/	device /s/
3. teethe /ð/	teeth /θ/	8. relieve /v/	relief /f/
4. excuse /z/	excuse /s/	9. grieve /v/	grief /f/
5. use /z/	use /s/	10. advise /z/	advice /s/

2 Practice saying the words you circled.

G Pair work: Which sentence contains the word?

Student A: Say the underlined word from sentence **a** or sentence **b**.

Student B: Say the sentence that contains that word.

Example

Student A: Proof

Student B: Bring proof tomorrow.

1. a. Can you <u>prove</u> it?
   b. Bring <u>proof</u> tomorrow.

2. a. Good <u>advice</u> is worth more than gold.
   b. I <u>advise</u> you not to go.

3. a. I <u>believe</u> you.
   b. "<u>Belief</u>" means "faith."

4. a. What <u>excuse</u> did they give?
   b. <u>Excuse</u> me.

5. a. I want to <u>save</u> money.
   b. Did you put your money in the <u>safe</u>?

6. a. This medicine should <u>relieve</u> the pain.
   b. The good news was a <u>relief</u> to me.

H Pair work: Dialogue with voiced sound /z/ and voiceless sound /s/

1 Practice saying these phrases. Be careful to make the vowels before final voiced consonants extra long.

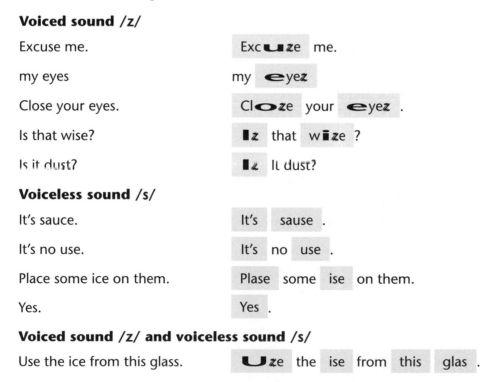

Voiced sound /z/

Excuse me.	Exc**u**ze me.
my eyes	my **e**yez
Close your eyes.	Cl**o**ze your **e**yez .
Is that wise?	**I**z that w**i**ze ?
Is it dust?	**I**z It dust?

Voiceless sound /s/

It's sauce.	It's sause .
It's no use.	It's no use .
Place some ice on them.	Plase some ise on them.
Yes.	Yes .

Voiced sound /z/ and voiceless sound /s/

Use the ice from this glass.	**U**ze the ise from this glas .

2 Practice this dialogue with a partner.

Trouble at the Restaurant

Customer:	Excuse me, waiter!
Waiter:	Yes? What's the matter?
Customer:	There's something in my eyes.
Waiter:	Is it dust?
Customer:	No, it's sauce!
Waiter:	It's no use rubbing them. Close your eyes and place some ice on them.
Customer:	Is that wise?
Waiter:	Yes! Use the ice from this glass.

I Pair work: Giving directions

1 Practice the street names on the map on page 116.

Student A: Say the name of a street on the map.
Student B: Point to that street.

Take turns saying the names of the streets.

2 Take turns saying each of these sample directions to your partner.

1. It's on the corner.
2. Turn east when you get to Leaf Avenue.
3. Go straight down Lag Street until you get to White Avenue. Then turn left.
4. It's on the left-hand side.
5. It's opposite the entrance to Oakley Mall.
6. Did you say "White" or "Wide"?
7. It's in the middle of the block.
8. From here, go two blocks north on Pace Drive.
9. It's on Sunrace Avenue.
10. Go west one block and then turn right on Sunrays.

Pair work: Map game

Each partner must have a copy of the map on page 116. One partner will be the "tourist" who is visiting a town. The other partner will be the "local" who lives in the town.

1 Local: Look at the list of places. Choose a location on the map for each place. Using a pencil, write the number of each place next to one of the drawings on your map. Do not show your map to the Tourist.

2 Tourist: Look at your map. Ask the Local how to get to one of the places on the list.

3 Local: Give clear directions to the place starting from the arrow marked "Start Here." Don't use your hands to show the Tourist where the place is.

4 Tourist: Use your finger or a pencil to follow the directions on your map. Mark the spot where you think the place is located.

5 Local: Check to see if the Tourist found the right place. After you give directions for three places, erase your numbers and change roles.

6 The new Local now chooses where to number the places, and the new Tourist now asks for directions.

Example

Tourist: Can you please tell me how to get to the Oakley Mall?

Local: Sure. Go two blocks north on Wide Avenue, and turn left on Leaf.

Tourist: Did you say "Leave"?

Local: No, "Leaf." After you turn left on Leaf, go west until you reach Lag Street. Oakley Mall will be on your right.

Tourist: (Mark the place that you found.)

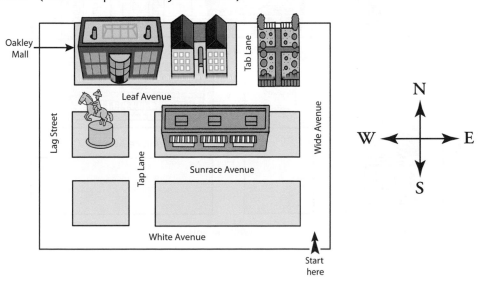

List of Places

1. Oakley Mall
2. Historical Society
3. Jazz Museum
4. Fine Arts Museum
5. Observation Tower
6. Hotel Oakley
7. Founder's Monument
8. Hall of Justice
9. Discount Delight Mall
10. Zoo
11. Botanical Gardens
12. Oakley Theater

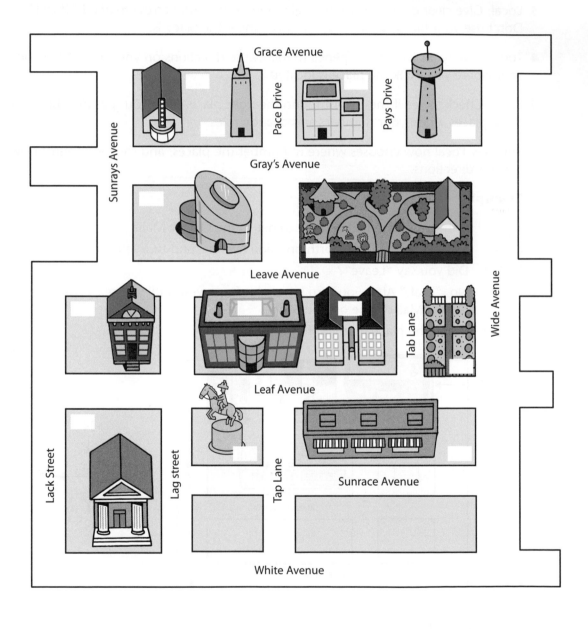

K Check yourself: Dialogue with voiced sound /z/ and voiceless sound /s/

Read the following dialogue. If possible, record the dialogue by yourself or with a partner. Listen to the recording. Did you lengthen the vowels before voiced consonants?

Where's the Zoo?

Tourist:	Could you please tell me how to get to the zoo from here?
Local:	Sure. Just go straight up Lack Street until you get to Leave Avenue.
Tourist:	Did you say "Leaf"?
Local:	No, no. "Leave." Then turn right on Leave, and go another two or three blocks, and you'll be right in front of the main entrance.
Tourist:	I appreciate the help. Thanks.
Local:	No problem. Enjoy the zoo.

L Review: Linking ☺☺☺

Practice linking in these sentences. Say each sentence several times until the combination of the last two words sounds like a new word.

1. We don't fear ice.   rice

2. Where does the trail end?   lend

3. Please use ink.   zinc

4. Can we save Anne?   van

5. What is there to laugh at?   fat

M Dictation

Listen and write the sentences you hear.

1. What kind of seat is this?

2.

3.

4.

5.

Aspiration: Contrasting voiced and voiceless stop sounds

In English, stop sounds at the beginning of a stressed syllable have an extra signal. This is important because it helps your listener notice the stress.

The **voiceless** stops /p/, /t/, and /k/ always have a small puff of air when they occur at the beginning of a stressed syllable. This is called *aspiration*. **Voiced** stops (/b/, /d/, and /g/) never have aspiration. You can help your English listener understand you more easily if you use aspiration for a voiceless stop at the beginning of a word or stressed syllable.

Listen. Practice saying the following pairs of words. There is a small ʰ to help you remember when to make the aspiration.

NOTE: You can check yourself by saying each word with a thin piece of paper in front of your lips. The paper will move if there is an extra puff of air. You can also feel the extra puff if you hold your hand in front of your mouth.

Voiceless stop /pʰ/	Voiced stop /b/
1. pay	bay
2. pan	ban
3. pea	bee
4. pole	bowl
5. peach	beach

Voiceless stop /tʰ/	Voiced stop /d/
6. tab	dab
7. tank	dank
8. teen	dean
9. ten	den
10. tied	died

Voiceless stop /kʰ/	Voiced stop /g/
11. cap	gap
12. cave	gave
13. coast	ghost
14. curl	girl
15. card	guard

O Aspiration in multi-syllable words

At the beginning of a stressed syllable, voiceless stops are always aspirated.

The stressed syllable in each word below begins with a voiceless stop. Practice saying the words. Be sure to make a puff of air after each stop at the beginning of stressed syllables.

/pʰ/	/tʰ/	/kʰ/
popular	**ten**sion	**ca**sual
pencil	**toast**ed	**co**ffee
a**ppear**	a**ttend**	a**ccuse**
a**part**ment	a**ttempt**	e**con**omy
re**port**	re**turn**	re**call**
un**pop**ular	e**ter**nal	un**cov**er

P Pair work: Aspiration in sentences

Student A: Say sentence **a** or sentence **b**.
Student B: Say the matching response.

Be sure to make a puff of air for each voiceless stop.

Example

Student A: Where's the peach?
Student B: In the fruit bowl.

1. a. Where's the peach?   In the fruit bowl.
   b. Where's the beach?   By the ocean.

2. a. Define "tank."   A container for liquid.
   b. Define "dank."   It means cold, wet, and unpleasant.

3. a. What does "tense" mean?   Under stress.
   b. What does "dense" mean?   Very thick.

4. a. How do you spell "could"?   C - O - U - L - D.
   b. How do you spell "good"?   G - O - O - D.

5. a. Where's the card?   In my desk.
   b. Where's the guard?   Standing at the door.

6. a. How do you spell "ghost"?   G - H - O - S - T.
   b. How do you spell "coast"?   C - O - A - S - T.

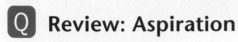 **Review: Aspiration**

Aspiration helps English listeners recognize the voiceless stop sounds at the beginning of stressed syllables.

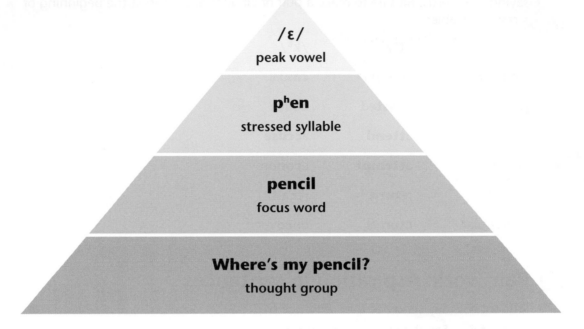

/ɛ/
peak vowel

pʰen
stressed syllable

pencil
focus word

Where's my pencil?
thought group

VOWEL WORK

 The spelling -ou- pronounced /aʷ/ as in "house"

The letters **-ou-** are pronounced **/aʷ/** about 81% of the time. This is the same sound as the vowel in "cow."

1 Listen and repeat these words.

cow /aʷ/		
house	proud	account
loud	sound	blouse
out	about	outfit
south	around	thousand
mouth	aloud	shout

2 Practice saying these sentences.

1. They found a house.
2. What's that loud sound?
3. She went outside and walked around the block.

14 | Sibilants

🎧 A | Introducing sibilants

Sibilants are consonants that make a hissing sound. This hissing sound comes from air rushing through a narrow V shape in the speaker's tongue. It is like wind through a narrow valley.

1 Listen to the following words. Each one ends in a different sibilant. Notice how all the sibilants make a hissing sound. The voiceless sibilants have a louder hiss.

| **Voiced sibilants** | his /z/ | beige /ʒ/ | badge /dʒ/ |
| **Voiceless sibilants** | hiss /s/ | wash /ʃ/ | batch /tʃ/ |

2 Look at the pictures below.

/s/ **and** /z/   /ʃ/ **and** /ʒ/

Looking from the side

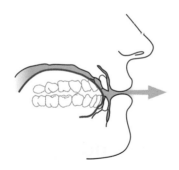 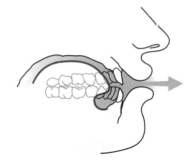

Looking down

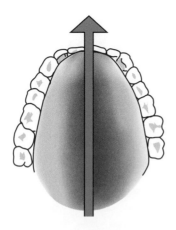 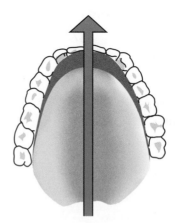

B Saying sibilants

1 To say /s/, press the sides of your tongue against your side teeth to form a valley down the center of your tongue. If you blow strongly, the air will rush through this narrow valley and make a high-pitched hissing noise as it goes past your front teeth.

The /ʃ/ sound is a little different. After whispering /s/ several times, move your tongue back just a little. Now there is more room for air to get out. With this position, the hissing noise will rush through the narrow valley with a lower pitch.

Make the /s/ and the /ʃ/ sounds several times, at first quietly, then out loud. If you blow out strongly, the sound for /s/ will be a higher hiss, and the sound for /ʃ/ will be a lower hiss. If you round your lips for /ʃ/, the difference between the two sounds will be more obvious.

2 Try both of these sounds with voicing. The sounds will now become /z/ and /ʒ/.

C Contrasting voiceless sibilants /s/ (see) and /ʃ/ (she)

Listen and repeat these pairs of words.

Beginning sounds		Final sounds	
/s/	/ʃ/	/s/	/ʃ/
Sue	shoe	mass	mash
see	she	gas	gash
same	shame	mess	mesh
so	show	lease	leash

D Contrasting voiced sibilants /z/ (zoo) and /ʒ/ (Asia)

Listen and repeat these pairs of words.

Middle sounds	
/z/	/ʒ/
laser	leisure
closing	closure
pleasing	pleasure
Caesar	seizure

E Linking with voiceless sibilant /ʃ/

1 Practice saying the following words, linking the /ʃ/ sound to the vowel that comes next.

trash everywhere   trasheverywhere

rush of traffic   rushov traffic

cash only   cashonly

2 Practice linking in these sentences.

1. A gash is a deep cut.
2. There was a flash of lightning.
3. Crush all the trash into the can.
4. Dogs must be on a leash at all times.

F Contrasting /s/ (sick) and /θ/ (thick)

The voiceless -**th**- sound /θ/ is not a sibilant because the tongue is flat and relaxed, so there is no hissing sound. The /s/ sound makes a hiss because the air is forced through a narrow valley.

1 Look at these pictures.

sick /s/   **thick /θ/**

Looking from the side

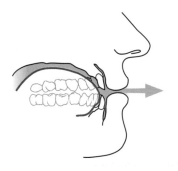
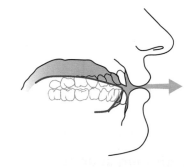

Looking to the front

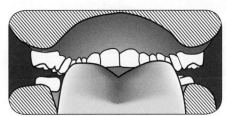
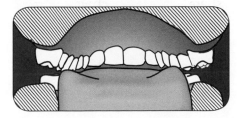

2 Listen and repeat these pairs of words.

Voiceless beginning sounds		Voiceless final sounds	
/θ/	/s/	/θ/	/s/
think	sink	math	mass
thank	sank	faith	face
thick	sick	myth	miss
thought	sought	mouth	mouse

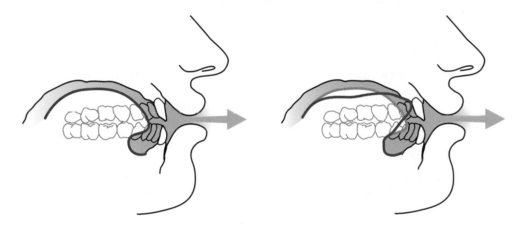 G Contrasting /ʃ/ (ship) and /tʃ/ (chip)

The sibilant **/tʃ/**, as in "chip," is pronounced as a combination of the stop sound **/t/**, followed by the continuant sound **/ʃ/**.

1 Look at these pictures.

ship /ʃ/   **chip /tʃ/**

Looking from the side

2 Listen and repeat these pairs of words.

Beginning sounds		Final sounds	
/ʃ/	/tʃ/	/ʃ/	/tʃ/
share	chair	wish	witch
shoe	chew	dish	ditch
sheep	cheap	mush	much
shop	chop	cash	catch

H Contrasting /dʒ/ (jet) and /y/ (yet)

The sibilant /dʒ/, as in "jet," is pronounced as a combination of the stop /d/, followed by the continuant /ʒ/. The positions for /dʒ/ are the same as for /tʃ/ as in "chip," but with voicing. The sound /y/, as in "yes," is not a sibilant.

1 Listen and repeat these words beginning with the /dʒ/ sound.

Joe	joy	just	juice
jar	jury	job	jump
judge	jam	Jack	jewel

2 Listen and repeat these words beginning with the /y/ sound.

yes	young	year	yard
you	your	yet	yellow
yell	yesterday	you'll	yoke

3 Say these pairs of words.

/dʒ/	/y/
jell	yell
Jell-O®	yellow
joke	yoke
jet	yet
jail	Yale
jewel	you'll

I Pair work: Contrasting /ʃ/, /tʃ/, /dʒ/, and /y/ in sentences

Student A: Say sentence **a** or sentence **b**.
Student B: Say the matching response.

NOTE: The sentences continue on the next page.

Example

Student A: What did you wash?
Student B: My car.

1. a. What did you watch?   An old movie.
   b. What did you wash?   My car.

2. a. What does "chatter" mean?   To talk fast.
   b. What does "shatter" mean?   To break into small pieces.

3. a. What's a "chip"?   A small piece.
   b. What's a "ship"?   A big boat.

4. a. What does "cheap" mean?   Not expensive.
   b. What does "jeep" mean?   A car for rough roads.

5. a. What's a joke?   Something funny.
   b. What's a yolk?   The yellow part of an egg.

6. a. Her son went to Yale.   That's wonderful!
   b. Her son went to jail.   That's terrible!

7. a. What's Jell-O®?   A kind of dessert.
   b. What's yellow?   A banana.

8. a. What does "jell" mean?   To become solid.
   b. What does "yell" mean?   To shout.

J Linking with /tʃ/ and /dʒ/ ⧉

1 Practice saying these words. Link the **/tʃ/** and **/dʒ/** sounds to the vowel sound that comes next.

catch it   catchit

match everything   matcheverything

Judge Anderson   JudgeAnderson

2 Practice linking in these sentences.

1. How can you watch every news program?
2. Try to catch it!
3. She wore a badge on her shirt.
4. The judge announced his choice.

K Music of English ♪

1 Listen. Notice the number of syllables in "oranges" and "slices."

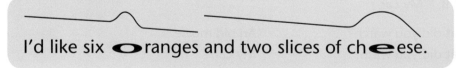

I'd like six ○ranges and two slices of ch⊖ese.

2 Listen again and repeat the sentence until you can say it easily.

L The -es ending and the number of syllables □ □ □

1 Listen to the following words that end in **-es**. In some of these words the **-es** ending adds an extra syllable, but in others it does not.

□	□ □	□	□ □
loves	prices	miles	causes
phones	dishes	homes	matches
cakes	freezes	dates	washes
bites	misses	leaves	judges

2 Do you know the rule for when the **-es** ending adds an extra syllable? If not, read the following clue.

Clue: Circle the words above that have a sibilant before the **-es** ending. How many syllables are in each word you circled?

3 Write down what you think the rule is when there should be an extra syllable with the **-es** ending. Check your answer on the bottom of page 130.

Rule: ....

M Pair work: Sibilants and the number of syllables □ □ □

Student A: Say a word from each pair of words below and on the next page.
Student B: Say the other word in the pair.

Example

Student A: Washes.
Student B: Wash.

NOTE: In most English words, the letter **-x-** is pronounced as a combination of the sound **/k/** followed by the sound **/s/**. So words ending in **-x-**, like "mix" and "box," have a final sibilant sound.

Voiceless sibilants   **Voiced sibilants**

□	□ □	□	□ □
wash	washes	rose	roses
ice	ices	cause	causes
dish	dishes	buzz	buzzes
watch	watches	badge	badges
rich	riches	quiz	quizzes
mix	mixes	judge	judges
tax	taxes	page	pages

N Pair work: Singular or plural?

Student A: Say a sentence with either the singular or the plural form of the word in parentheses.

Student B: Say "singular" or "plural."

Example

Student A: The match fell on the floor.

Student B: Singular.

1. The (match / matches) fell on the floor.
2. Did you see the (prize / prizes)?
3. What (excuse / excuses) did he make?
4. Where did you put the (box / boxes)?
5. It depends on the (price / prices).
6. Did you wash the (dish / dishes)?
7. I put the (rose / roses) in water.
8. Which (sentence / sentences) did you write?

O Pair work: Dialogue

Listen. Then practice saying the dialogue with a partner.

Prizes

(A couple is talking at home. The wife has an idea, but her husband isn't very excited about it.)

Wife:	Do you like surprises?
Husband:	Sometimes. What is it?
Wife:	We have a chance to win some great prizes.
Husband:	How? Go on a TV quiz show?
Wife:	You guessed it! I decided it would be fun.
Husband:	I'm no good at quizzes.
Wife:	But the second prize is a new watch!
Husband:	I don't need any more watches.
Wife:	And the first prize is a million dollars!
Husband:	That's not so great. You have to pay a lot of taxes on prize money.

P. Review: Linking with /ʃ/, /tʃ/, and /dʒ/ 🔗

Practice linking in these sentences. Say each sentence several times until the linked sounds seem like a new word.

1. The stain won't wash out.   shout

2. You can't catch air.   chair

3. How much does the judge owe?   Joe

Q. Tongue twisters with /s/, /z/, /ʃ/, and /θ/

Listen to these tongue twisters. Then practice saying them.

1. She is certain to show you the sailors from the ship.

2. She sells seashells by the seashore.

3. Miss Beth Smith saw a mouse in the path.

R. Check yourself: Sibilants and the number of syllables ☐ ☐ ☐

1 If possible, record yourself reading these sentences.

I'd like six oranges and two slices of cheese. Oh . . . And may I have seven boxes of dates, please? One large and six small.

2 Listen to your recording, and check if you said the right number of syllables. Did you have an extra syllable for "oranges," two syllables for "slices" and "boxes," and one syllable for "dates"?

S. Dictation

Listen and write the sentences you hear.

1. Please don't put ice in my water. ....

2. ....

3. ....

4. ....

5. ....

VOWEL WORK

 Difficult vowel contrasts

Listen and repeat these difficult vowel contrasts.

tea /iʸ/	is /ɪ/
reach	rich
steal	still
feel	fill
heel	hill
we'll	will

cake /eʸ/	ten /ɛ/
chase	chess
fade	fed
shade	shed
age	edge
tail	tell

ten /ɛ/	pan /æ/
dead	dad
head	had
then	than
end	and
lend	land

pan /æ/	top /ɑ/
add	odd
jab	job
stack	stock
band	bond
backs	box

Answer to Task L (page 127)

3 *Rule*: The **-es** ending adds an extra syllable only when it comes after a sibilant.

15 Thought Groups

 A Introducing thought groups

1 As you learned in Unit 6, you must emphasize the most important words – focus words – to help your listeners understand what you mean. Focus words are emphasized by:

   1. Making the vowel in the stressed syllable of the focus word extra long and extra clear.

   2. Adding a pitch change to the stressed syllable.

2 Another way that you can help your listeners understand you better is by separating words into **_thought groups_**. A thought group can be a short sentence or part of a longer sentence. Each thought group has a focus word.

   Listen. The following sentence has three main points of information. That makes three thought groups with three focus words and, therefore, three peaks of melody.

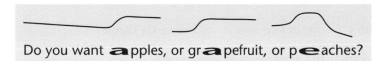

Do you want **a**pples, or gr**a**pefruit, or p**e**aches?

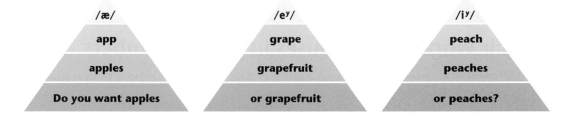

/æ/	/eʸ/	/iʸ/
app	grape	peach
apples	grapefruit	peaches
Do you want apples	or grapefruit	or peaches?

 B Signaling the end of a thought group with a pause

A **_pause_** gives your listeners time to think about what was just said. If people have trouble understanding you, pausing at the end of each major thought group can help them understand you better.

NOTE: In written sentences, punctuation marks such as commas, periods, and question marks are often used to indicate the pause at the end of a thought group.

1 Listen to these sentences. Notice how pauses are used between the thought groups.

   1. I'd like six oranges, and two slices of cheese.
   2. When you get there, call me, and I'll come get you.
   3. "Let's go for a walk," I said. But she replied, "I'm busy."

2 Practice saying the sentences. Pause after each thought group.

C Using pauses with numbers

A pause is especially important when you are saying numbers (in addresses, telephone numbers, and so on). When numbers are written, each group is separated by a space or by punctuation marks, like parentheses or dashes. Notice how spaces and punctuation are used to group the numbers in the following phone number.

(415) 555-6963

In speech, pauses can be used to show how the numbers are grouped.

1 Listen to these numbers.

55-56963	five five	five six nine six three
555-6963	five five five	six nine six three

Did you hear the difference in grouping?

2 Practice saying the numbers above.

D Pair work: Using pauses in phone numbers

Different countries group phone numbers differently. This is how phone numbers are grouped in the United States:

Area code	Local code	Personal number
315	555	7131

1 Student A: Say phone number **a** or **b**. Be sure to pause at the end of each group.

Student B: Write what you hear. Then check with your partner to find out if you wrote the correct number.

1. a. (9165) 555-031
  b. (916) 555-5031 ....

2. a. (86) 555-5627
  b. (865) 55-5627 ....

3. a. (6055) 55-589
  b. (60) 555-5589 ....

2 Student A: Say your own telephone number, or one you make up, to your partner.

Student B: Write what you hear.

Your partner's phone number: ....

Did you write the number with the correct grouping?

E Pair work: Using pauses in math problems

Student A: Say math problem **a** or **b**. Be sure to pause at the end of each grouping of numbers, as shown below.

Student B: Circle the math problem that you hear. Then say the correct answer.

Examples

Student A: $(3 \times 3) + 5 =$ what?

> three times three   plus five   equals what?

Student B: 14

Student A: $5 - (2 \times 2) =$ what?

> five   minus two times two   equals what?

Student B: 1

Math problem	Answer
1. a. $(3 \times 3) + 5 =$ what?	14
b. $3 \times (3 + 5) =$ what?	24
2. a. $(5 - 2) \times 2 =$ what?	6
b. $5 - (2 \times 2) =$ what?	1
3. a. $(4 - 1) \times 3 =$ what?	9
b. $4 - (1 \times 3) =$ what?	1
4. a. $(10 - 1) \times 2 =$ what?	18
b. $10 - (1 \times 2) =$ what?	8
5. a. $(4 + 2) \times 3 =$ what?	18
b. $4 + (2 \times 3) =$ what?	10
6. a. $(2 \times 2) + 3 =$ what?	7
b. $2 \times (2 + 3) =$ what?	10

Signaling the end of a thought group with a falling pitch

A falling pitch is another signal that a thought group is finished. Often a falling pitch and a pause are used together to signal the end of a thought group. However, when a speaker is talking quickly, there may not be time for a pause between thought groups. Then it is especially important to use a falling pitch.

1 Listen and repeat these sentences. Use a falling pitch as well as a pause to signal the end of each thought group.

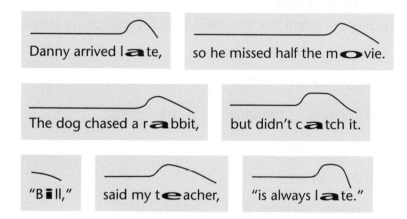

Danny arrived l**a**te,

so he missed half the m**o**vie.

The dog chased a r**a**bbit,

but didn't c**a**tch it.

"B**i**ll,"

said my t**ea**cher,

"is always l**a**te."

2 Practice these math problems again using a pause as well as falling pitch to signal the end of each group.

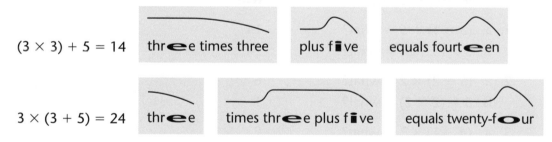

$(3 \times 3) + 5 = 14$ thr**ee** times three   plus f**i**ve   equals fourt**ee**n

$3 \times (3 + 5) = 24$ thr**ee**   times thr**ee** plus f**i**ve   equals twenty-f**ou**r

> ## Thought Group Rule 2
> There is often a fall in pitch at the end of a thought group to signal that the thought group is finished.

NOTE: A small fall in pitch means the end of the thought group. A big fall means the end of a sentence (or getting ready to start a new topic). A *very* big fall means the end of a person's turn to speak.

G Pair work: Signaling the end of a thought group

Student A: Say sentence **a** or **b**. Then ask the question underneath the two sentences.

Student B: Respond with the appropriate answer on the right.

Example

Student A: "John," said the boss, "is absent."
             Who was speaking?

Student B: The boss.

1. a. John said, "The boss is absent."   John.
    b. "John," said the boss, "is absent."   The boss.
        Question: Who was speaking?

2. a. Alfred said, "That clerk is incompetent!"   Alfred.
    b. "Alfred," said that clerk, "is incompetent!"   That clerk.
        Question: Who was speaking?

3. a. The teacher said, "That student is intelligent."   The teacher.
    b. "The teacher," said that student, "is intelligent."   That student.
        Question: Who was speaking?

4. a. Lisa said, "My sister is taller."   Lisa.
    b. "Lisa," said my sister, "is taller."   My sister.
        Question: Who is speaking?

H Either/or questions

Either/or questions offer a choice. Each choice belongs to a separate thought group. The pitch often rises on the first choice, but rises and falls on the second choice. This helps make the two choices clear.

Listen to these either/or questions. Notice how the pitch rises on the first choice, and then rises and falls on the second choice. Also notice the pause between the two choices.

I Asking either/or questions

Practice saying these questions. Let the pitch rise on the first choice, and then rise and fall on the second choice.

1. Would you like to work or rest?
2. Was the movie good or bad?
3. Is the chain silver or gold?
4. Will you go by bus or by train?
5. Do you want soup or salad?

J A series of items

When a sentence contains a series of items, each item is a separate thought group. There is often a rise in pitch on each item in the series. However, on the final item in the series, the pitch rises and then falls. That means "the end."

Listen to the following sentences. Notice how the pitch rises for each item of the series and then falls on the last item.

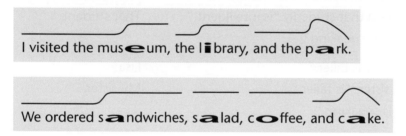

K Saying a series of items

Practice saying these sentences. Be sure to let the pitch rise and fall on the last item in each series.

1. The fabric is red, blue, and yellow.
2. We're going to Chicago, Toronto, and then New York.
3. The zoo has elephants, tigers, bears, and lions.
4. His suitcase contains socks, ties, shirts, and some books.
5. We need forks, knives, spoons, and cups.
6. I'm studying economics, history, biology, and geography.

L Pair work: Identifying thought groups

Student A: Say either sentence **a** or sentence **b**. Then ask the question underneath the two sentences.

Student B: Respond with the appropriate answer on the right.

Take turns saying the sentences and asking the questions.

Example

Student A: Do you want soup or salad?

How many things were you offered?

Student B: Two.

1. a. Do you want a Super Salad?   One.
    b. Do you want a soup or salad?   Two.
        Question: How many things were you offered?

2. a. Jane said, "Is that Mister Fogg?"   A person.
    b. Jane said, "Is that mist or fog?"   The weather.
        Question: What was Jane asking about?

3. a. He sold his house, boat, and car.   Three.
    b. He sold his houseboat and car.   Two.
        Question: How many things did he sell?

4. a. She likes pie and apples.   Apples.
    b. She likes pineapples.   Pineapples.
        Question: What kind of fruit does she like?

5. a. We used wooden matches to start the fire.   One.
    b. We used wood and matches to start the fire.   Two.
        Question: How many things did they use?

6. a. She collects golden coins.   One.
    b. She collects gold and coins.   Two.
        Question: How many types of things does she collect?

Pair work: Dialogue using focus words in a series of thought groups

1 Listen to the following dialogue, and make a slash (/) at the end of each thought group. Then underline the focus word in each thought group.

Difficult Children

Mother:	We want a turkey and cheese <u>sandwich</u>, / and two tuna sandwiches.
Server:	On white, whole wheat, or rye?
Mother:	The turkey and cheese on rye, and the other two on whole wheat.
Daughter:	No! No! I want white bread!
Mother:	Whole wheat's good for you.
Son:	I want peanut butter and jelly, not tuna!
Mother:	OK. One turkey and cheese on rye, one tuna on white, and one peanut butter and jelly.
Server:	What would you like to drink?
Mother:	One iced tea and two glasses of milk.
Daughter:	No milk! Lemonade!
Mother:	Three sandwiches, one iced tea, and two glasses of water.

2 Check your partner's slashes. Did you agree on where to put pauses? Practice the dialogue with your partner. Use pauses and pitch to make the thought groups clear.

Check yourself: Dialogue practice with thought groups

1 Read the following dialogue, and make a slash (/) where you think each thought group ends. Then underline the focus word in each thought group. There is one focus word in each thought group.

Coffee Shop Confusion

(The customer doesn't hear very well, and the server is impatient.)

Customer: What can I have to <u>start</u> with? /

Server: <u>Soup</u> / or <u>salad</u>. /

Customer: What's Super Salad?

Server: What do you mean, "Super Salad"?

Customer: Didn't you say you have a Super Salad?

Server: No, we don't have anything like that. Just plain green salad.
Or you can start with tomato soup.

Customer: Oh, OK. Well, what do you have for dessert?

Server: We have ice cream, pie, and apples.

Customer: I don't like pineapples very much.

Server: Are you making jokes or what? We have ice cream, pie, and apples.

Customer: OK, OK. Just give me the soup and a piece of apple pie.

Server: Sorry, the only pie we have is berry.

Customer: Very what?

Server: Excuse me?

Customer: You said the pie was very something. Very good?

Server: I said the pie was berry – blackberry! And if you will wait just a minute,
I'm going to get another server for you.

2 Practice the dialogue with a partner. Remember to use pauses and pitch to make the thought groups clear.

3 If possible, record the dialogue and then listen to it. Were the separate thought groups made clear? Were the focus words emphasized?

O Analyzing a sentence

1 Fill in each level of pyramids 1 and 2 using the two thought groups in this sentence:

   Is it harder to speak or to listen?

2 This sentence has two thought groups. Put the first thought group in the bottom of the first pyramid and the second thought group in the bottom of the second pyramid.

3 Find the focus word of each thought group and put each focus word in the third level of each pyramid.

4 Find the stressed syllable of each focus word and put each stressed syllable in the second level of each pyramid.

5 Find the peak vowel of each stressed syllable and put each peak vowel symbol in the top level of each pyramid. (You can find the vowel symbols on page xvi.)

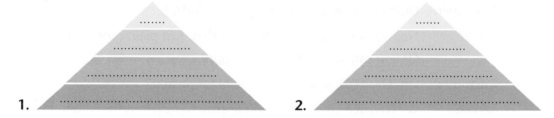

1.   2.

P Review: Focus and thought groups

In the future, if someone has difficulty understanding what you have said, try following these steps.

1. Identify the focus words in what you just said. (**soup** or **salad**)

2. Think about which syllable is stressed in each focus word. (**sal**ad)

3. Say the sentence(s) again, but make sure that you:

  • Lengthen the vowel in the stressed syllable of each focus word. (slad)

  • Make the sounds in the stressed syllable of each focus word very clear. (s**æ**lad)

  • Change pitch on the stressed syllable of each focus word.

salad

  • Group your words together in thought groups by using pitch changes (rises or falls) and by using pauses.

  Do you want soup or salad?

  • End complicated or especially important thought groups with an extra long pause, so the listener will have more time to think about what you just said.

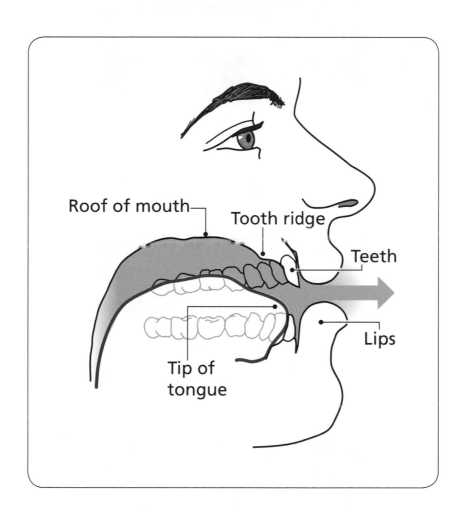

Roof of mouth

Tooth ridge

Teeth

Lips

Tip of tongue

Appendix B
Tongue Shapes for /s/ or /z/, /t/ or /d/, /θ/ or /ð/, /r/, and /l/

Looking to the front

/s/ or /z/

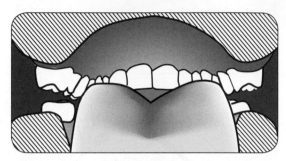

/t/ or /d/

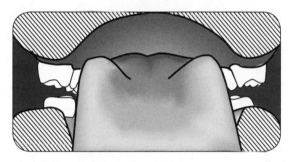

/θ/ or /ð/

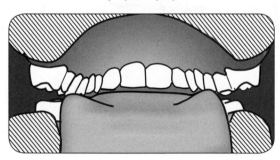

/r/

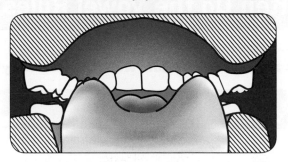

/l/

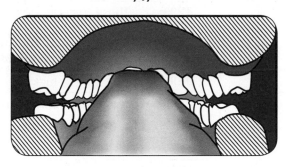

Looking down

/s/ or /z/   /t/ or /d/   /θ/ or /ð/

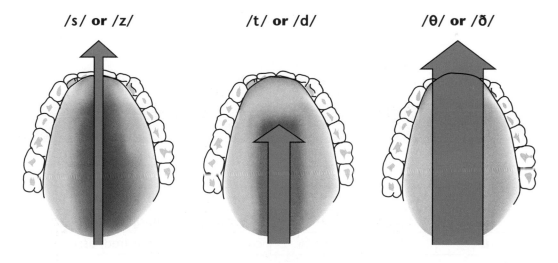

Appendix C
How Often Do the Vowel Rules Work?

How often does the Two Vowel Rule work in stressed syllables?

Letters	Sounds	Percent of time[1]	Examples
-ai-	/e^y/	95%	rain, afraid, acquaint, sailor
-a- + final **-e-**		90%	cake, came, arrange
-ay-		93%	day, play, array, delay, betray
-e- + final **-e-**	/i^y/	32%	these, recede, delete
-ee-		98%	tree, speech, asleep, agreement
-ea-		69%	tea, please, beat, season
-y-[2]		95%	city, funny, lucky
-i- + final **-e-**	/ɑ^y/	77%	ice, time, define, arrive, admire
-igh-[2]		100%	night, light, high, sigh
-o- + final **-e-**	/o^w/	76%	cone, home, alone
-oa-		94%	coat, soap, approach, floating
-ow-[2]		53%	slow, below, lower, flowing
-u- + final **-e-**	/u^w/	94%	blue, juice, duty, conclude
-oo-[2]		88%	room, choose, foolish

How often does the One Vowel Rule work in stressed syllables?

Letters	Sounds	Percent of time[1]	Examples
-a-	/æ/	91%	pan, has, aspirin, answer, attraction
-e-	/ɛ/	82%	ten, credit, message, medicine, intention
-i-	/ɪ/	93%	is, simple, children, interesting
-o-	/ɑ/	74%	top, hot, problem, opposite, confident
-u-	/ʌ/	66%	cup, sun, butter, hundred, assumption

---

[1] Source: *A Survey of English Spelling*, Edward Carney, Routledge, London, 1994. These percentages of times that these spellings produce these vowel sounds are based on analyses of a database of 2.5 million words in British and American dictionaries.

[2] NOTE: **-y-**, **-igh-**, **-ow-**, and **-oo-** do not actually fit the Two Vowel Rule but are included because they are so often pronounced with these vowel sounds. However, a few common **-oo-** words, like "good" and "foot," are pronounced with the vowel sound /ʊ/.

Extra Practice 1
More Consonant Work

Part 1   /r/ and /l/

A Listening to /r/ and /l/

1 Listen to the final sound in each word.

car   call   mire   mile   fear   feel

2 Listen to the beginning sound in each word.

row   low   rhyme lime   rain   lane

B Saying /r/ and /l/

The sounds **/r/** as in "fear" and **/l/** as in "feel" are both continuants. When pronouncing **/r/**, air flows out along the middle of the tongue without stopping. Do not let the tip of your tongue touch the roof of your mouth. For **/l/**, the tip of the tongue touches the tooth ridge at the front of the mouth, and air flows out each side.

1 Look at these pictures to see the differences between **/r/** and **/l/**.

fear /r/   feel /l/

Looking from the side

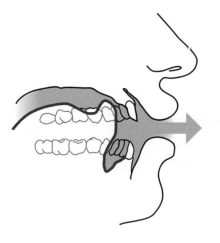
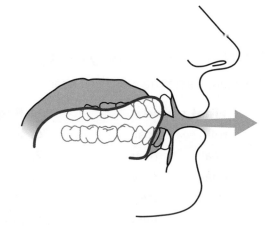

Looking to the front

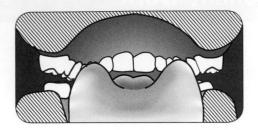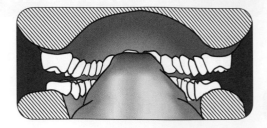

Looking down

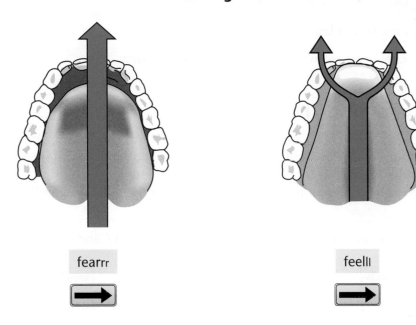

fearrr	feelll

2 Whisper the words "fear" and "feel" several times. Then practice saying them out loud.

∩ C Which word do you hear?

1 Listen. Circle the word you hear.

Final sound		**Beginning sound**	
1. (roll)	roar	6. (lock)	rock
2. heal	(hear)	7. (low)	row
3. (coal)	core	8. late	(rate)
4. steel	(steer) استي	9. lamb	(ram)
5. fail	(fair)	10. (lime)	rhyme

2 Practice saying the words you circled.

D Pair work: Saying /r/ and /l/ in sentences

Student A: Ask question **a** or question **b**.
Student B: Say the matching answer.

Take turns asking the questions.

Example

Student A: What's a lamb?
Student B: A baby sheep.

1.	a. What's a ram?	A male sheep.
	b. What's a lamb?	A baby sheep.
2.	a. Is it fall?	No, it's still summer.
	b. Is it far?	No, it's close.
3.	a. Is it light?	No, it's heavy.
	b. Is it right?	No, it's wrong.
4.	a. What does "core" mean?	The center, like the middle of an apple.
	b. What does "coal" mean?	A black rock that can burn.
5.	a. What does "pale" mean?	Lacking color.
	b. What does "pair" mean?	A set of two.
6.	a. How do you spell "lane"?	L - A - N - E.
	b. How do you spell "rain"?	R - A - I - N.

E Linking with /r/ and /l/

Practice linking with these sentences.

1. They moved far away.   They moved farrraway .

2. Park the car on the street.   Park the carrron the street.

3. Call everyone!   Calllleveryone !

4. How do you feel about this?   How do you feelllabout this?

5. Tear it out!   Tearrrit out.

6. We'll always remember.   We'llllalways remember.

F Poem with /r/ and /l/

Practice saying this poem. Be careful to say the **/r/** and **/l/** sounds clearly.

The Crocodile

How doth the little crocodile
Improve his shining tail,
And pour the waters of the Nile
On every golden scale!

How cheerfully he seems to grin!
How neatly spreads his claws,
And welcomes little fishes in
With gently smiling jaws!

– Lewis Carroll

NOTE: "Doth" is an old word for "does." "Scales" are small bony flakes covering some fish and reptiles.

Part 2 /n/ and /l/

A Listening to /n/ and /l/

1 Listen to the final sound in each word.

ten   tell   mine   mile   win   will

2 Listen to the beginning sound in each word.

no   low   night   light   need   lead

B Saying /n/ and /l/

The sounds /n/ and /l/ are both continuants. When saying the sound /l/, air flows out of the mouth around each side of the tongue. When saying the sound /n/, air does not flow out of the mouth. Instead, it flows out of the nose.

1 Look at these pictures to see the differences in tongue position and airflow for the sounds /n/ and /l/.

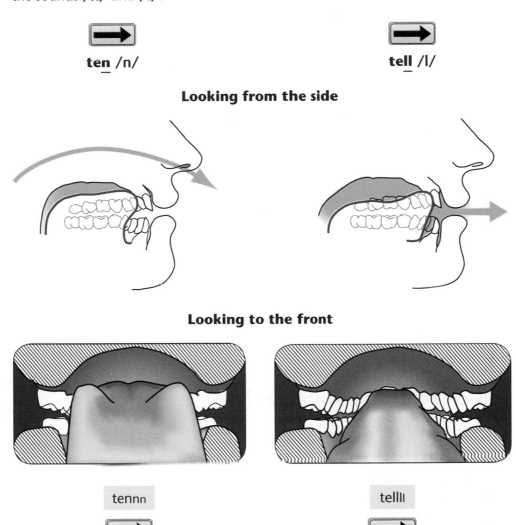

ten /n/   tell /l/

Looking from the side

Looking to the front

tennn   tellll

2 Practice the positions for /n/ and /l/. Then whisper the words "ten" and "tell" several times. Pay attention to the difference in airflow for the final sounds.

3 Practice saying "ten" and "tell" out loud.

C The mirror test

You can use a mirror to check if you are saying the sounds /**n**/ and /**l**/ correctly.

1 If you have a small mirror, follow these steps.

   1. Hold the mirror under your nose, and say the sound /**n**/ strongly.
   2. Quickly look at the mirror, and you should see a cloud.

   3. Say the sound /**l**/ and quickly look at the mirror. This time you should not see a cloud.

2 Try the mirror test with these words. Check your mirror after each word.

seen	seal
ten	tell
fine	file
rain	rail

D Which word do you hear?

1 Listen. Circle the word you hear.

Final sound		**Beginning sound**	
1. (pine)	pile	6. name	lame
2. cone	coal	7. nice	lice
3. main	mail	8. knife	life
4. when	well	9. niece	lease
5. tune	tool	10. not	lot

2 Practice saying the words you circled.

E Pair work: Saying /n/ and /l/ in sentences

Student A: Ask question **a** or question **b**.

Student B: Say the matching answer.

Example

Student A: What does "croon" mean?

Student B: A kind of singing.

1. a. What does "croon" mean?   A kind of singing.
   b. What does "cruel" mean?   Unkind.

2. a. What's the opposite of "night"? Day.
   b. What's the opposite of "light"? Heavy.

3. a. How do you spell "snow"?   S - N - O - W.
   b. How do you spell "slow"?   S - L - O - W.

4. a. Can you define "snack"?   It's something to eat between meals.
   b. Can you define "slack"?   It's the opposite of "tight."

5. a. What's a tool?   A piece of equipment.
   b. What's a tune?   A song.

F The sound combinations /nd/ and /ld/

Each of the following words ends in the sound combination **/nd/** or **/ld/**. Listen and repeat each pair of words. Be careful to say the **/n/** and **/l/** sounds clearly.

/nd/	/ld/	/nd/	/ld/
find	filed	mind	mild
phoned	fold	spend	spelled
trained	trailed	found	fouled

G Linking with /n/, /l/, and /d/

Practice linking with these sentences.

1. They can always go.   They   cannnalways   go.
2. We call our dad every Sunday. We   callllour   dadevery   Sunday.
3. We called our boss.   We   calledour   boss.
4. When are you coming?   Whennnare   you coming?
5. Don't spend all our cash.   Don't   spendallllour   cash.

Part 3 /v/ and /w/

A Listening to /v/ and /w/

Listen to the beginning sound in each of these words.

vine   wine   veil   whale   vile   while

B Saying /v/ and /w/

The sounds /v/ as in "vine" and /w/ as in "wine" are both continuants. When saying /v/, the upper teeth touch the back of the lower lip. For /w/ the lips are very rounded, and the teeth do not touch the lips at all.

1 Look at these pictures to see the differences in teeth and lip position for the sounds /v/ and /w/.

<u>v</u>ine /v/   <u>w</u>ine /w/

Looking from the side

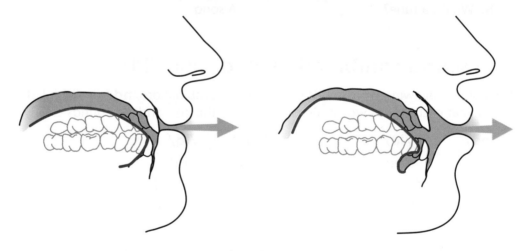

2 Practice alternating between the positions for /v/ and /w/. Then whisper the words "vine" and "wine" several times. Pay attention to the beginning sound in each word.

3 Practice saying "vine" and "wine" out loud.

C Which word do you hear?

1 Listen. Circle the word you hear.

1. vile   (while)
2. vent   went
3. verse   worse
4. veal   wheel
5. vain   wane
6. vicious   wishes
7. -v-   we
8. vest   west

2 Practice saying the words you circled.

D Pair work: Saying /v/ and /w/ in sentences

Student A: Ask question **a** or question **b**.
Student B: Say the matching answer.

Example

Student A: What does "vain" mean?
Student B: Conceited.

1. a. What does "vain" mean?   Conceited.
   b. What does "wane" mean?   To get weaker.

2. a. Where's the wine?   In the bottle.
   b. Where's the vine?   On the fence.

3. a. How do you spell "whale"?   W - H - A - L - E.
   b. How do you spell "veil"?   V - E - I - L.

4. a. Where's the vest?   In the closet.
   b. Where's the West?   Opposite the East.

5. a. How do you spell "wishes"?   W - I - S - H - E - S.
   b. How do you spell "vicious"?   V - I - C - I - O - U - S.

6. a. Is he a very old man?   No, only 55.
   b. Is he a wary old man?   Yes, very suspicious.

7. a. What does "vile" mean?   Nasty.
   b. What does "while" mean?   A length of time.

Part 4   /v/ and /b/

🎧 A Listening to /v/ and /b/

1 Listen to the final sound in each of these words.

rove   robe   curve   curb

2 Listen to the beginning sound in each of these words.

vase   base   vote   boat

B Saying /v/ and /b/

The sound **/v/** is a continuant and **/b/** is a stop. When saying **/v/**, the upper teeth touch the back of the lower lip. The lips do not touch each other, and this allows air to flow out of the mouth. When saying **/b/**, the lips close, stopping the air inside the mouth.

1 Look at these pictures to see the differences between **/v/** and **/b/**.

rove /v/   **robe /b/**

Looking from the side

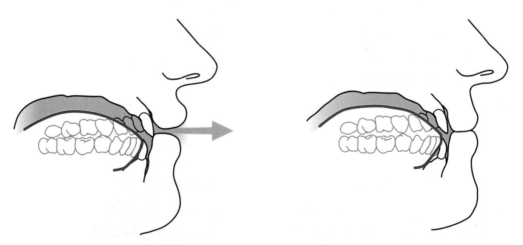

2 Silently try the positions for these two sounds.

NOTE: If you have trouble keeping your lips apart for the **/v/** sound, place a pencil or your finger under your upper lip to remind you to keep the lips apart.

3 Practice whispering the words "rove" and "robe." Then practice the words out loud.

C Which word do you hear?

1 Listen. Circle the word you hear.

Beginning sound		**Final sound**	
1. vase	(base)	**6.** rove	robe
2. vat	bat	**7.** curve	curb
3. very	berry	**8.** carve	carb
4. van	ban	**9.** dove	dub
5. vest	best	**10.** jive	jibe

2 Practice saying the words you circled.

D Pair work: Saying /v/ and /b/ in sentences

Student A: Say sentence **a** or sentence **b**.

Student B: Say the matching response.

Take turns saying the sentences.

Example

Student A: He wants to buy my vote.

Student B: That's against the law!

1. a. He wants to buy my boat.   Will you sell it?
       b. He wants to buy my vote.   That's against the law!

2. a. What's a bat?   A stick used in baseball.
       b. What's a vat?   A big container for liquid.

3. a. What does "vest" mean?   A jacket with no sleeves.
       b. What does "best" mean?   The qreatest.

4. a. Where's the vase?   On the table.
       b. Where's the base?   On the bottom.

5. a. What does "marvel" mean?   An amazing thing.
       b. What does "marble" mean?   A kind of stone.

6. a. What's a curve?   A bend.
       b. What's a curb?   The edge of a street.

E Linking with /v/ and /b/ ⬡⬡⬡

Practice linking with these sentences.

1. Will you leave early?   Will you leavvvearly ?
2. Have a bite.   Havvva bite.
3. Can you believe it?   Can you believvvit ?
4. Don't rob us!   Don't robus !
5. Join the club again.   Join the clubagain .
6. It won't rub off.   It won't ruboff .

F Pair work: Saying /v/ and /b/ in a dialogue

Practice this dialogue with a partner.

The Great Athlete

A: Do you like to play volleyball?
B: Not very much.
A: But it's fun!
B: I can't serve the ball.
A: You just have to keep working at it.
B: But I never get the ball over the net.
A: Never?
B: Well, hardly ever. Besides that, I always bump into the other players.
A: Hmm. Then maybe you'd better try bowling.

Part 5   /f/ and /p/

A Listening to /f/ and /p/

Listen to the difference between these words.

leaf   leap   coffee   copy   fool   pool

B Saying /f/ and /p/

1 Look at these pictures for the continuant sound **/f/** and the stop sound **/p/**. The teeth, tongue, and lip positions for these sounds are the same as for **/v/** and **/b/**, but **/f/** and **/p/** are voiceless.

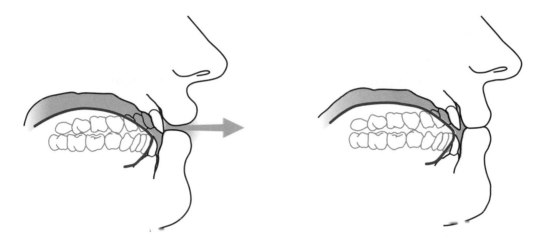

leaf /f/   leap /p/

Looking from the side

2 Silently practice the positions for **/f/** and **/p/**. Then whisper the words "leaf" and "leap" several times.

3 Practice saying "leaf" and "leap" out loud.

∩ C Which word do you hear?

1 Listen. Circle the word you hear.

Beginning sound		Final sound	
1. fool	(pool)	**7.** laugh	lap
2. fast	past	**8.** wife	wipe
3. foot	put	**9.** cliff	clip
4. foal	pole	**10.** leaf	leap
5. fat	pat	**11.** beef	beep
6. face	pace	**12.** chaff	chap

2 Practice saying the words you circled.

D Pair work: Saying /f/ and /p/ in sentences

Student A: Say sentence **a** or sentence **b**.
Student B: Say the matching response.

Take turns asking the questions.

Example

Student A: Where's the pan?
Student B: In the kitchen cabinet.

1. a. Where's the fan?   On the ceiling.
   b. Where's the pan?   In the kitchen cabinet.

2. a. What's the opposite of "fail"?   "To succeed."
   b. What's the opposite of "pale"?   "Bright and colorful."

3. a. What's a fool?   A silly person.
   b. What's a pool?   A place to swim.

4. a. What's a foal?   A baby horse.
   b. What's a pole?   A long stick.

5. a. How do you spell "wife"?   W - I - F - E.
   b. How do you spell "wipe"?   W - I - P - E.

6. a. How do you spell "lab"?   L - A - B.
   b. How do you spell "laugh"?   L - A - U - G - H.

7. a. The copy machine doesn't work.   Call the technician.
   b. The coffee machine doesn't work.   I guess I'll have tea.

E Linking with /f/ and /p/ ⌾⌾⌾

Practice linking with these sentences.

1. There's a leaf in your hair.   There's a   leaffin   your hair.

2. If it fits, I'll wear it.   Ifffit   fits, I'll wear it.

3. Stuff all the clothes in this bag.   Stufffall   the clothes in this bag.

4. Leap over the fence.   Leapover   the fence.

5. Clip important articles.   Clipimportant   articles.

6. I like to sleep until seven.   I like to   sleepuntil   seven.

Part 6 /θ/ and /t/

A Listening to /θ/ and /t/

1 Listen to the final sound in each of these words.

bath   bat   both   boat

2 Listen to the beginning sound in each of these words.

thank   tank   thought   taught

B Saying /θ/ and /t/

The sound **/θ/** as in "bath" is a continuant, and the sound **/t/** as in "bat" is a stop.

1 Look at these pictures of **/θ/** and **/t/** and notice how the air flows out of the mouth for **/θ/**, but stops inside the mouth for **/t/**.

bath /θ/

bat /t/

Looking from the side

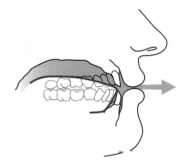

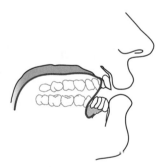

Looking to the front

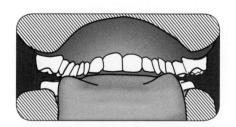

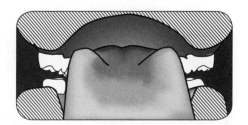

When saying **/θ/**, the tongue is flat and relaxed. The flat tip of the tongue briefly touches the upper front teeth. You can also make this sound by touching the tip of the tongue to the lower front teeth. Either way, the air must continue to flow out of the mouth.

2 Silently practice the position for **/θ/**. Breathe out and feel the air moving quietly over the tongue and teeth. If you draw the air back into your mouth, you can feel the cold air over your flat tongue.

3 Raise your tongue and press it against the tooth ridge all around so that the air cannot flow out. This makes the stop sound **/t/**.

4 Silently change back and forth between the positions for the two sounds. Then practice saying the words "bath" and "bat" out loud.

C Which word is different?

Listen. You will hear three words. Mark the column for the word that is different.

	X	Y	Z	
1.	....	....	.......✔.......	(bath, bath, bat)
2.	....	....	....	
3.	....	....	....	
4.	....	....	....	
5.	....	....	....	
6.	....	....	....	
7.	....	....	....	
8.	....	....	....	

D Pair work: Saying words with final /θ/ and /t/

Student A: Say one word from each pair of words.

Student B: Pay attention to the final sound in the word, and say "stop" or "continuant."

Example

Student A: Bath.

Student B: Continuant.

	→	STOP
1.	bath	bat
2.	both	boat
3.	booth	boot
4.	faith	fate
5.	Ruth	root
6.	math	mat
7.	wrath	rat

E Pair work: Saying sentences with /θ/ and /t/

Student A: Say sentence **a** or sentence **b**.
Student B: Say the matching response.

Take turns asking the questions.

Example

Student A: What does "path" mean?
Student B: A little road.

1. a. What does "path" mean?   A little road.
   b. What does "pat" mean?   To tap.

2. a. What's a bath for?   To get clean.
   b. What's a bat for?   To play ball.

3. a. How do you spell "both"?   B - O - T - H.
   b. How do you spell "boat"?   B - O - A - T.

4. a. What does "faith" mean?   Belief.
   b. What does "fate" mean?   Destiny.

5. a. How do you spell "mat"?   M - A - T.
   b. How do you spell "math"?   M - A - T - H.

6. a. Define "wrath."   It means anger.
   b. Define "rat."   It's like a big mouse.

7. a. Where is the booth?   At the fair.
   b. Where is the boot?   On my foot.

8. a. How do you spell "Ruth"?   R - U - T - H.
   b. How do you spell "root"?   R - O - O - T.

Part 7   Silent -*t*- and reduced -*t*-

🎧 A   Silent -*t*-

When the phrases "want to" and "going to" are said quickly, the "to" is often reduced so much that the letter -**t**- is silent. When "want to" is said quickly, it often sounds like "wanna." When "going to" is said quickly, it often sounds like "gonna."

NOTE: You do not need to use this reduction when you speak English, but you should learn to recognize it in other people's speech.

Listen and write the missing words you hear.

1. We ....*want to*....... go on a trip.
2. I .... buy a car.
3. They .... buy a present.
4. I think they're .... leave.
5. Are you .... show us your work?
6. What are you .... do now?
7. I .... study now.
8. Why do you .... work so hard?
9. Because I .... succeed.
10. Is she .... be rich now?

B   Reduced -*t*- between vowels

At the end of a stressed syllable, the letter -**t**- is often reduced to a quick /**d**/ sound when it is followed by a vowel. For example, the word "liter" sounds like "leader," and the word "atom" sounds like "Adam."

NOTE: Practicing saying the reduced -**t**- will help you hear it accurately when you listen to other speakers.

Practice using a quick /**d**/ sound for the letter -**t**- in the following words and phrases.

later	atom
water	great ending
better	short answer
liter	hit another
hotter	write in
city	get us

Part 8   Practice with linking

A   Review: Linking with stops

Practice linking stops to vowels in these sentences.

1. We made other plans.
2. Lock all the doors.
3. Stop it now!
4. They got away.

5. Rob always goes.
6. I'll bet it doesn't fit anymore.
7. Dave bought a bag of chips.
8. Would anyone like a cup of tea?

B   Linking with the same continuant sound

When you link two continuant sounds that are the same, do not say the sound twice. Instead, say the sound once, but make it longer.

1 Practice saying these linked words.

bus system	bussssystem
half full	halffffull
team member	teammmmmember

2 Practice linking with these sentences. Do not pause between the linked words.

1. Pam might go. | Pammmmight go.
2. The sun never rises this early. | The sunnnnneverrrrises this early.
3. Bill loves to dance. | Billllloves to dance.
4. We both think it's beautiful.
5. I wish she'd come.

C   Review: Linking with different continuant sounds

Practice linking with continuants in these sentences.

1. This is a space age project.
2. That's a fair answer.
3. You can't have both of them.
4. We can always share a taxi.

5. He'll always be there Monday.
6. There's a fly in this ice!
7. Please answer my question honestly.
8. I'm never there on Saturdays.

Extra Practice 2
Advanced Tasks

Part 1   Word stress

A   Pair work: Practice with syllable number and word stress

Student A: Ask question **a** or question **b**.
Student B: Say the matching answer.

Pay attention to the stressed syllables in bold.

Example

Student A: What's the train like?
Student B: It's fast and loud.

1. a. What's the te**rrain** like?   It's very hilly.
   b. What's the **train** like?   It's fast and loud.

2. a. What does "**sport**" mean?   A game, like football.
   b. What does "su**pport**" mean?   Something like "help."

3. a. What color is "**rust**"?   Reddish brown.
   b. What color is "**russ**et"?   More brown than red.

4. a. How do you spell "**sett**ing"?   S - E - T - T - I - N - G.
   b. How do you spell "**sting**"?   S - T - I - N - G.

5. a. How do you spell "**fast**"?   F - A - S - T.
   b. How do you spell "**fac**et"?   F - A - C - E - T.

6. a. What does "**tenn**is" mean?   A sport with rackets.
   b. What does "**tense**" mean?   In this class, it's a grammar word.

7. a. What does "**planned**" mean?   The past tense of "plan."
   b. What does "**plan**et" mean?   A thing that goes around the sun.

8. a. Was it **wrapped**?   Yes, in wrapping paper.
   b. Was it **rap**id?   No, very slow.

9. a. What does "**stamped**" mean?   The past tense of "stamp."
   b. What does "stam**pede**" mean?   A lot of animals running wildly.

B Descriptive phrases and compound words

When an adjective comes just before a noun in a two-word descriptive phrase, the second word of the phrase (the noun) is stressed.

Adjective	Noun	Descriptive phrase
green	+ house	= green **house** (a house that is green)

However, when an adjective and a noun are combined to form a compound word, the stress is always on the first part of the compound word (the adjective).

Adjective	Noun	Compound word
green	+ house	= **green**house (a glass building used for growing plants)

Practice saying the following compound words and descriptive phrases with the correct stress patterns. The stressed syllables are in bold.

NOTE: Compounds are sometimes written as two words and sometimes as one.

Descriptive phrase		**Compound word**	
1. a white **house**	(a house that is white)	the **White** House	(the U.S. President's house)
2. a white **board**	(a board that is white)	a **white**board	(used for writing in class)
3. a black **bird**	(a bird that is black)	a **black**bird	(a specific type of bird)
4. a dark **room**	(a room without light)	a **dark**room	(a place to develop film)
5. a hot **dog**	(a warm animal)	a **hot** dog	(something to eat)

C Pair work: Saying stressed syllables in sentences

If you say words using their correct stress pattern, it is easier for other people to understand you, even if you do not get all the sounds exactly right.

Student A: Ask question **a** or question **b**.
Student B: Say the matching answer.

NOTE: The questions are on the next page.

Example

Student A: What did you think of the committee?
Student B: They're writing a good report.

1. a. What did you think of the com**mitt**ee?   They're writing a good report.
    b. What did you think of the **com**edy?   It wasn't very funny.

2. a. What does "**el**igible" mean?   Qualified.
    b. What does "il**leg**ible" mean?   Unreadable.

3. a. Does she want a **need**le?   Yes, to sew on a new button.
    b. Does she want **any** doll?   No, she wants a special one.

4. a. Do the students like **his**tory?   No, there are too many dates.
    b. Do the students like his **stor**y?   Yes, it's funny.

5. a. How do you spell "**dep**uty"?   D - E - P - U - T - Y.
    b. How do you spell "the **beau**ty"?   T - H - E   B - E - A - U - T - Y.

6. a. Is it ele**men**tary?   No, it's advanced.
    b. Is it a **lem**on tree?   No, it's an orange tree.

7. a. What's for **rain**?   An umbrella.
    b. What's **for**eign?   Another language.

8. a. What's in the **des**ert?   Lots of sand.
    b. What's in the de**ssert**?   Lots of sugar.

Part 2   Sentence focus

A **Pair work: Focus words and the meaning of emphasis**

Student A: Say sentence **a** or sentence **b**. Be sure to emphasize the focus word.

Student B: Listen closely for the focus word and say the response that best matches the sentence you hear.

Example

Student A: We want three tickets for to**day's** show.

Student B: Not tomorrow's show.

1. a. We want **three** tickets for today's show.   Not two.
    b. We want three tickets for to**day's** show.   Not tomorrow's show.

2. a. Please give me **both** books.   Not just one.
    b. **Please** give me both books.   I want them very much.

3. a. I didn't know she was out **there**.   I thought she was somewhere else.
   b. I didn't know **she** was out there.   I thought it was someone else.

4. a. I **think** I paid five dollars.   I'm not sure.
   b. I think I paid **five** dollars.   Not ten.

5. a. I told **you** about that.   I didn't tell anyone else.
   b. I **told** you about that.   Don't you remember?

6. a. Gary **lives** here.   He's not just visiting.
   b. Gary lives **here**.   Not somewhere else.

7. a. John ordered **co**ffee!   Not tea.
   b. **John** ordered coffee!   Not me

B Pair work: Focus words in a dialogue

1 Working alone, underline the focus words in this dialogue.

2 Take turns reading the dialogue out loud to your partner. As you listen to your partner, circle the words your partner emphasizes.

NOTE: You and your partner do not have to agree on your choice of focus words, but you do have to make your choice of focus words clear by emphasizing them with a pitch change and a long, clear vowel in the stressed syllable.

New York Cab Ride

Driver: Where to?

Passenger: Times Square, please.

Driver: Where are you visiting from?

Passenger: Chicago.

Driver: Yeah, that's what I thought, from the accent.

Passenger: Really? I have an accent? Funny, I never thought about it. Where are you from?

Driver: Atlanta.

Passenger: Really? You're from the South? You don't sound southern.

Driver: No, of course not. I'm studying to be an actor, and you can't have any accent if you want to be an actor.

Passenger: So you just got rid of your southern accent?

Driver: That's right. I wiped it out completely.

Passenger: That's really interesting. I guess that's why you sound like you're from New York.

Driver: I do?

C Pair work: Checking information

In the following dialogues, Speaker B emphasizes a question word ("how," "what," "why," etc.) to find out what Speaker A said. This is a useful way to ask about something you did not understand or did not hear clearly.

A: Millie let the cat out!
B: **Who** did?
A: Millie.

A: The sandwich was made with goat cheese.
B: **What** kind of cheese?
A: Goat cheese.

1 Read each dialogue. Write a question for Speaker B that makes sense with Speaker A's final answer.

1. A: We need tomatoes for the sauce.
   B: What do we need_____?
   A: Tomatoes.

2. A: Tom needs a new battery for his car.
   B: _____?
   A: Tom.

3. A: The travel agent made a mistake in our arrangements.
   B: _____?
   A: The travel agent.

4. A: Melissa is coming at five o'clock.
   B: _____?
   A: At five.

5. A: We went to the airport by bus.
   B: _____?
   A: By bus.

6. A: Richard has a mountain of books on his desk.
   B: _____?
   A: On his desk.

7. A: You need a badge to get into the building.
   B: _____?
   A: A badge.

2 Practice reading the dialogues out loud with your partner.

D Pair work: What was the question?

When listening to a conversation, you may not hear everything that is said. For example, you may hear a speaker's response without hearing the question that came before it. When this happens, if you listen closely to the emphasis in the response, you may be able to guess what the question was.

1 Read the dialogues below and fill in Speaker A's missing question. Then compare your questions with your partner. Your questions may not be exactly the same, but they should make sense with Speaker B's final answer.

1. A: When does the train leave?

   B: At seven.

   A: _Seven in the morning_____?

   B: No, in the **eve**ning.

2. A: When will you begin your vacation?

   B: In June.

   A: ....?

   B: No, at the **end** of June.

3. A: How much will a ticket cost?

   B: Twenty dollars.

   A: ....?

   B: No, **twen**ty.

4. A: What are those people doing?

   B: They're planting a garden.

   A: ....?

   B: No. A **veg**etable garden.

5. A: What's the play about?

   B: The Revolution.

   A: ....?

   B: No, the **French** Revolution.

6. A: Where will they hold the meeting?

   B: In Washington.

   A: ....?

   B: No, in Washington **State**.

2 Practice reading the dialogues out loud with your partner.

E What will come next?

Using correct emphasis when you speak can help your listener predict what you will say next. This will make it easier for your listener to follow what you are saying.

1 Read the unfinished sentences below and predict what the speaker will say next. Write an ending to each sentence, and underline the word or words that should be emphasized (the focus word) in the part that you wrote.

1. We had a lot of rain **last** year, but <u>not much this year</u>.

2. I don't like to **write**, but ....

3. **This** pen doesn't write very well, but ....

4. To**ma**toes are expensive, but ....

5. My **sis**ter got a raise in pay, but ....

6. Brian is really **tall**, but ....

2 Practice saying the sentences. Be careful to emphasize only the focus words.

Part 3 Thought groups

A Road signs

Road signs are words or phrases that tell your listener that you will either continue talking about the same idea or that you are going to change direction. In other words, road signs let your listener know where you are headed, so that the listener can follow what you are saying.

Road signs are important signals. They should be said with a pitch change and a pause, so that the listener will notice them.

1 The following words and phrases tell the listener that the speaker will continue in the same direction.

first of all	secondly	moreover	and then
besides	as a result	consequently	so
furthermore	in the same way	in addition	in fact

2 Read these sentences and notice how road signs are used to guide the listener.

First of all, you should be well prepared.

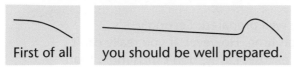

Secondly, it's essential that you arrive on time.

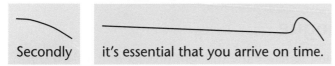

3 The following words and phrases tell the listener that the speaker will not continue in the same direction, but will change direction.

| however | instead | on the contrary | in contrast |
| but | nevertheless | on the other hand | yet |

4 Notice how a road sign is used in this sentence.

However, if you really can't be on time, have a good excuse.

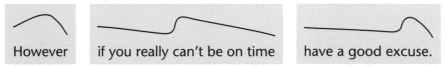

5 The following words and phrases let the listener know that the speaker is about to finish.

| lastly | finally | to sum up |
| all in all | in conclusion | to conclude |

6 Read this sentence and notice how a road sign is used.

Lastly, don't miss more than three classes.

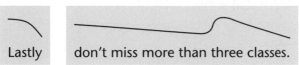

7 Practice reading the following paragraph out loud. Be sure to separate the thought groups clearly. Be extra careful to use pitch changes and pauses with the road signs.

> First of all, you should be well prepared. Secondly, it's essential that you arrive on time. However, if you really can't be on time, have a good excuse. Lastly, don't miss more than three classes.

B Pair work: Monologue

1 Read the following story and separate the thought groups with a slash (/). Remember to draw a slash after each road sign.

2 Underline the words that should be emphasized (the focus words) in each thought group.

A Bad Day

This has been the most terrible day! Everything went wrong! First of all, I couldn't find my keys. Then, I knew I was going to be late to work, so I drove too fast, and a cop gave me a speeding ticket. When the officer asked for my driver's license, I realized that I had left it at home! As a result, the fine will be even higher. After that, I got a flat tire and had to change it, which took even more time. Finally, when I arrived at work, I remembered that it was a holiday, and the office was closed!

3 Take turns listening to each other tell the story. Did you emphasize the focus words? Did you use pitch changes and pauses to help the listener follow the story? Could you recognize the pitch changes and pauses when your partner was telling the story?

C Parenthetical remarks

Parenthetical remarks carry information that is less important. In writing, they are marked by parentheses, dashes, or commas. In speech, they are usually said at a lower pitch and marked by pauses on either side.

Read the following sentences with the pitch pattern shown.

1. Students, of course, should be well prepared.

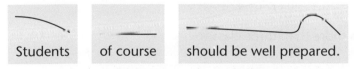

2. Unprepared students (naturally) get less out of their classes.

| Unprepared students | naturally | get less out of their classes. |

3. They find – to their surprise – that effort does pay off.

| They find | to their surprise | that effort does pay off. |

D Pair work: Road signs and parenthetical remarks

1 Underline the road signs with double lines and the parenthetical remarks with single lines in the following passage.

Preparing for a Job Interview

A job interview, as you probably know, can be a pretty stressful experience. However, there are several things you can do to help ensure that an interview will run smoothly.

First of all, prepare yourself by learning as much as you can about the job you are applying for. Look for information about the company or organization online, for example, or speak to others who work in the same field.

Secondly, make a list of your relevant skills and experiences. Write down those things you have learned in school, for instance, or in other jobs that will help you be successful in the position you hope to fill. Then, try to memorize the skills and experiences you listed, so that you can refer to them easily during the interview.

On the day of the interview, leave yourself more than enough time to get there. You should try to arrive early or, at the very least, get there on time. After all, you do not want to rush into the meeting or, even worse, arrive late.

Finally, try not to be nervous. This, of course, is the hardest step of all. However, if you have made an effort to prepare yourself adequately, then you have every reason to approach the interview with complete confidence.

2 Take turns reading the passage out loud to your partner. Be sure to use pauses and the appropriate pitch changes with each road sign and parenthetical remark. Did your partner hear your pauses and pitch changes?

Credits

Illustrations

Judith Alderman: 77 (*looking to the front*), 85 (*looking to the front*), 90 (*looking to the front*), 123 (*looking to the front*), 142, 143 (*looking to the front*), 146 (*looking to the front*), 149 (*looking to the front*), 159 (*looking to the front*); **Patty Blau:** 73; **Judy B. Gilbert:** 28 (*man*); **Adam Hurwitz:** xi, 2, 3, 10, 11, 18, 22, 23, 24, 28 (*map*), 44, 51 (*hands*), 57, 76, 77 (*looking from the side*), 78, 80, 84, 85 (*looking down*), 90 (*looking from the side, down*), 101, 109, 110, 121, 123 (*looking from the side*), 124, 141, 143 (*looking down*), 145, 146 (*looking down*), 149 (*looking from the side*), 150, 152, 154, 157, 159 (*looking from the side*); **Chris Reed:** 41, 48, 58, 97 (*snake, bee*), 100, 114, 115, 116, 128, 138, 148; **Andrew Shiff:** 51 (*musician*), 93, 97 (*woman*)

Photo

iii ©Tetra Images/Getty Images

Text

The author and publisher are grateful for permission to reprint the following item: 73 "The Hippopotamus," in *I'm a Stranger Here Myself*, by Ogden Nash, 1938, Little, Brown and Co. Reprinted by permission of Curtis Brown, Ltd. Copyright © 1935 by Ogden Nash. Also in *Collected Poems*, by Ogden Nash, Andre Deutsch, Ltd.

Class and Assessment Audio CD Theme Music

"Lone Jack to Knob Noster" by Jack Rummel from his CD, *Lone Jack: The Ragtime of Today.*